COUNTERING HITLER'S SPIES

This book is dedicated to Colin James Robinson, who was born on 26 November 1938 and sadly passed away on 15 July 2020. His life was well lived and was one that saw him loved by many. He was a great grandfather of 8, a grandfather of 7, a father to Susan, Colin, Gary and Scott, a husband to Wynn, and a good friend to many more.
Gone but not forgotten.

COUNTERING HITLER'S SPIES

British Military Intelligence
1940–1945

STEPHEN WYNN

Pen & Sword
MILITARY

AN IMPRINT OF PEN & SWORD BOOKS LTD.
YORKSHIRE – PHILADELPHIA

First published in Great Britain in 2020 by
PEN & SWORD MILITARY
An imprint of
Pen & Sword Books Ltd
Yorkshire - Philadelphia

ISBN 978 1 52672 552 3

A CIP catalogue record for this book is available from the British Library

Typeset in Ehrhardt MT & 12/16
by SJmagic DESIGN SERVICES, India.
Printed and bound in the UK by TJ International Ltd.

Pen & Sword Books Ltd incorporates the imprints of Pen & Sword Archaeology,
Atlas, Aviation, Battleground, Discovery, Family History, History, Maritime,
Military, Naval, Politics, Social History, Transport, True Crime, Claymore Press,
Frontline Books, Praetorian Press, Seaforth Publishing and White Owl

For a complete list of Pen & Sword titles please contact

PEN & SWORD BOOKS LTD
47 Church Street, Barnsley, South Yorkshire, S70 2AS, England
E-mail: enquiries@pen-and-sword.co.uk
Website: www.pen-and-sword.co.uk

Or

PEN & SWORD BOOKS
1950 Lawrence Rd, Havertown, PA 19083, USA
E-mail: Uspen-and-sword@casematepublishers.com
Website: www.penandswordbooks.com

Contents

Introduction

Much has been written about spies and military intelligence throughout the course of the Second World War, with information and disinformation being used to distort and cover up what was really going on, or what was actually going to take place. Although the Second World War was ultimately won on the battlefield, in the air and the sea, with the spilling of the blood of brave men, military intelligence also played its part; in fact it played a massive part in ending the war sooner than it would have otherwise done.

It was achieved by a combination of spies – the individuals who were in place and actually carried out the dangerous tasks of acquiring and passing the information – and their handlers who they answered to in the background; who did the thinking and planning of the operations and who knew what information was required.

The spies on the ground, who often worked behind enemy lines, required nerves of steel, regardless of the reasons behind what they were doing. All it took was for them to say one wrong word, be somewhere at the wrong time, or be betrayed by somebody they thought they could trust, or in some cases by individuals they didn't even know, and it was all over. Living with that constant fear and worry, day in and day out, took a special kind of person. It wasn't a role that just anybody could take on and for some it was simply too much of a burden to carry.

One of the most obvious of all questions is what made people become spies in the first place, as nearly all of them had little or no military experience. Some were ideological, some did it for money, some maybe had no choice because of threats made against them or their families by the German *Abwehr* (Military Intelligence Service), whilst others agreed to come to the UK as a way of escaping the clutches of the Nazis.

One thing seems to be apparent though, those who chose to become German spies, did not appear to be that good at it. By the end of the war many who had crossed the English Channel to carry out their clandestine work were no longer alive. For them, the price that they paid for their choice was as costly as it could possibly be.

This book looks at some of the individual stories connected with Germany's attempts at wartime espionage, and asks the question: how was it that the *Abwehr* had no idea that nearly all of their agents had been turned by the British? It also looks at the part MI5 played in all of this, especially with their use of the Double-Cross System, which was acclaimed as a total success, but was it? Read on and see what you think.

Chapter One

Four German Spies

On 23 May 1940, just thirteen days after Winston Churchill became the new British Prime Minister, having taken over from Neville Chamberlain, who had resigned, the Treachery Act came into being as law throughout the United Kingdom. Anybody who was charged and found guilty under the Act, was in serious trouble, as it only allowed for one punishment: death.

The reason for the Act being brought into law was down to Winston Churchill, as he believed that British efforts up to that point in the war had been thwarted from within and not because of the military superiority of Germany. Churchill received legal advice that if 'Fifth Columnists' did in fact exist and had been responsible for British military defeats, there could be a problem if any of those involved were foreign nationals. British nationals could be adequately dealt with under the Treason Act, but foreign nationals were exactly that, foreign, and not British, and therefore could not be tried for treason. That is why it took just thirteen days for the Treachery Act to be written up, passed through Parliament and given the Royal assent. This is quite possibly the shortest possible period of time it has ever taken for a law to find its way onto the statute books.

Whether the four young men who stepped ashore on the Kent coast in the early hours of Tuesday, 3 September 1940 knew of the Treachery Act and the danger they were now in, is unclear. The men in question were, **Carl Meier**, aged 23 and Dutch by birth; **Charles van den Kieboom**, aged 25 who, although born in Holland, had dual Dutch and Japanese nationality; **Sjoerd Pons**, another Dutchman aged 28 and a 25-year-old German who called himself **Jose Waldberg**. These men were not holiday makers who had decided to visit the United Kingdom for sight-seeing trips, bird watching and pleasure. Their purpose was to act as spies for the *Abwehr*. They were specifically meant to observe and report back about any and all movements along the south coast of England; this was in readiness for a supposed imminent invasion of Great Britain by German forces. The irony for the four men, of course, was that Hitler's supposed invasion never took place.

On landing on the Kent coast, they were to split up and carry out their observations across as much of southern England as possible. They each had in their possession a small radio transmitter, false documents and food supplies that were to last them for ten days. They were clearly not the brightest of individuals, either that, or the level of training they received from the *Abwehr* was of a poor standard; either way it beggars belief that they were actually operational spies. It is staggering that their spy masters seriously believed them to be of a suitable standard to be sent into the field to carry out such an important operation – but they did. Was that out of incompetence, arrogance, or was it a true reflection of just how badly run German military intelligence was?

The first to be captured was also the youngest of the group, 23-year-old Carl Meier. Having landed on the Kent coast he made his way inland and quickly arrived in the village of Lydd where, rather than keeping as low a profile, he walked straight into the village pub, the Rising Sun, where he stuck out like a sore thumb and immediately drew attention to himself. For a start, he was a stranger with a foreign accent, which always made people suspicious, especially with the nation at war and everybody on a heightened level of paranoia and on the lookout for anybody who looked or sounded like they might be a spy.

Meier walked into the pub at 9am and attempted to purchase alcohol, which wasn't possible at that time of the day. An Englishman would have known that and if the *Abwehr* had done their homework properly, they too would have also known that it was not possible to purchase alcohol in a British pub at that time in the morning – a basic error, but an extremely costly one for Meier.

It wasn't long before Meier, Waldberg, Pons and van den Kieboom were all arrested, which came about as a direct result of Meier walking into the Rising Sun public house and trying to purchase an alcoholic drink.

Although initially arrested by the local police, they were handed over to MI5 and transported to their main interrogation centre at Latchmere House, Ham in South London. There they spent six weeks being interrogated and telling their stories of what their purpose was in coming to England. Their interrogators were happy that they had more than sufficient evidence to charge all four men under the Treachery Act. Still probably oblivious as to their fate, they all appeared at Bow Street Magistrates court in London on 24 October 1940, where they were remanded in custody until the following month, to appear at the Central Criminal Court of the Old Bailey. Their appearance at court had been conducted under a blanket of the utmost secrecy, with only those who needed to know being allowed in court.

Security was even tighter when the matter was heard in Court One at the Old Bailey on 19 November 1940, as the prosecution requested the judge to evoke the Emergency Powers (Defence) Act, which banned the disclosure of any information with regard to any part of the proceedings. Just five months earlier, in June 1940, there had been an amendment made to the original Act of 1939, which stated that the Home Secretary could serve a notice on a newspaper not to report on a certain matter due to the potential threat to national security, with the allowance for the editor to appeal that decision before the courts if he so wished. But the June 1940 amendment (2d) greatly increased the Home Secretary's powers and provided him with absolute power to determine what constituted a potential threat to national security, to which there was no right of appeal.

On 31 July 1940, there was a lengthy and heated debate on this very point in the House of Commons, which is recorded in Hansard. The reason for the debate, which was brought before the House by Mr Samuel Silverman, the Member of Parliament for the constituency of Nelson and Colne, was the real concern that this provided the Home Secretary with too much power, allowing for a comparison to be made with Nazi Germany's Dr Goebbels.

Word quickly spread about the request for an order to be made under the Emergency Powers (Defence) Act in the proceedings that had begun in Court One, but no members of the Press were allowed in to hear anything to do with the case.

Of the four men, van den Kieboom, Meier and Pons, all pleaded not guilty of committing offences under the Treachery Act, but van den Kieboom and Meier were found guilty. Pons pleaded not guilty, telling the court he had no intention, nor had he done anything which had assisted Germany since he had arrived in England. He had been arrested by the German authorities for attempting to smuggle gems into the country from Holland. He had then been handed over to the *Abwehr* and only agreed to help them because they threatened to send him to a concentration camp and, although he didn't know the full horrors of life in those camps, he knew that it wasn't a place that he wanted to be. He then re-iterated the fact that he had never had any intention of assisting the *Abwehr*. Fortunately for Pons, the jury believed his story and after a trial that lasted for four days, they took less than ninety minutes to find him not guilty. He was set free by the judge, but then immediately re-arrested for being an enemy alien.

If that was a surprise, there was an even bigger one still to come for the fourth defendant, Waldberg, pleaded guilty. The only sentence available to the judge for those like Waldberg who pleaded guilty, or those who were found guilty by the jury, was the death penalty. Now, on the assumption that Waldberg was of sound mind and body and did not have a desire to die, the question has to be asked, why would he plead guilty to the offence if he knew that such a plea would cost him his life?

Prior to the trial Waldberg had been held at Pentonville Prison in London and whilst there he claimed that his name was not Jose Waldberg and that he was not German. He insisted that his name was in fact Henri Lassudry and he was Belgian. The initial response and belief from MI5 officers was that Waldberg had changed his story to save himself from an inevitable end. But his French was excellent and noted to be much better than his German, unless of course he was fluent in both languages and was simply pretending his grasp of German was poor to help his claim that he was a Belgian national.

In the days following the trial Waldberg and Meier were informed that they were to be hanged at 9am on 10 December 1940 at Pentonville prison. Kieboom was hanged a week later at the same location.

The secrecy surrounding the case had remained tightly in place and in the following days and weeks still nothing about it had leaked out in either the newspapers or on the radio.

After Waldberg had been informed of the date of his execution, he wrote a number of letters to his family, one of which was to his parents and another to his girlfriend. The one to his parents was addressed to Monsieur and Madame Lassudry, in the Rue des Colonies, in Brussels, Belgium, and his girlfriend, Helene Ceuppens, who lived in nearby Ixelles. If these people were real, then the British authorities potentially had a big problem on their hands, and not just because he was Belgian and not German. In one of the letters, Waldberg had written that the man representing him, a barrister by the name of Blundell, had advised him that his best course of action was to plead guilty to the charges against him, but for some reason he did not mention that the only sentence available to the judge for a guilty verdict, was the death sentence. Accepting that the claim was true, why Blundell had given such advice is a mystery and was clearly against his duty and responsibility to do his best for his client. Was he asked to do so by a higher authority?

For some reason Waldberg was not allowed to say anything in his own defence. He had intended to plead not guilty as his co-defendant Pons, his claim being that he was acting under duress because, having been arrested by the Gestapo, they then threatened to arrest his father if he did not agree to spy for them in England. It was a defence that had worked for Pons, so why not Waldberg?

As much as it is strange that Blundell gave Waldberg such poor advice, one struggles to understand why, despite his intention to plead not guilty, citing duress as his real reason for coming to England, he then allowed himself to be persuaded to change his plea to guilty. It does not make any sense at all. In his final letter to his mother, he told her the time and date that he was due to be executed, despite the fact that he had absolutely no idea if or when she would receive it.

There was a lot of controversy surrounding his situation. After Waldberg had been found guilty and sentenced to death, Colonel William Edward Hinchley-Cooke, who had worked for MI5 and its predecessor, the British Secret

Service, since August 1914 just after the outbreak of the First World War, was so uncomfortable with the situation that he went to see the then Attorney General, Sir Donald Somervell, to make his concerns known. He posed the question that now the man's true name and nationality had been discovered, whether it would not be better to stay his execution. Somervell was unmoved by Hinchley-Cooke's words and was unwilling to intervene in the matter.

Hinchley-Cooke was not the only person to have reservations about the executions. Sir Alexander Maxwell, a permanent under-secretary at the Home Office, was particularly concerned with not only the secrecy surrounding the case, but the speed in which the sentences had been handed down. It also didn't sit easy with him that the prosecutions had been carried out in complete secrecy, as had the decisions to sentence three of the men to death.

Winston Churchill had put in place a 'body' called the Security Executive to oversee MI5. The man in charge of them was Viscount Swinton and it was to him that Sir Alexander Maxwell wrote. His letter included the sentence, 'To carry out sentences of this kind in secrecy is contrary to all our traditions.'

There was however a difference between Hinchley-Cooke's concerns and Maxwell's. It would appear that the latter felt compelled to write to Swinton, not necessarily out of a genuine concern that an injustice might have taken place, but to ensure that when similar events took place in the future, if there was any blame to be handed out, that it should fall squarely at the feet of Swinton and MI5 and not the Home Secretary. Maxwell went as far as to suggest that Swinton write a letter on the matter so that the Home Office could keep it on their files; that way the Home Secretary would be exonerated if any negative press should come from a future such incident.

Swinton did in fact reply to Maxwell's letter, but it wasn't necessarily the answer he was looking for. In it he explained how MI5 had already managed to 'turn' a number of *Abwehr* agents against their own masters. In a case where the arrest or detention of an enemy agent had been seen and witnessed by a member of the public, or the agent had refused to be turned, they would be charged under the Treachery Act, and if found guilty, which they usually were, they would be summarily executed.

Swinton explained the 'Double-Cross' system to Maxwell, and outlined its structure of intelligence and counter-espionage, adding how important a part it played in the war effort, and that a single disclosure about just one individual who was part of the system, could bring an end to it all, which could add years to the war.

It was only after Meier and Waldberg had been executed that an official announcement of their capture, trial and execution was released to the Press:

> The two men had been apprehended shortly after their surreptitious arrival in this country, with a wireless set and a large sum of money; that they had been tried and convicted and had been hung that morning. Editors are asked not to press for any additional facts or to institute any inquiries.

Kieboom was executed in the same manner exactly a week later, which brought a similar communiqué from the Home Office, but no mention of Pons or his acquittal was ever made public.

Three observations about Waldberg are worthy of mention and are needed to fairly complete his story. Firstly, I believe MI5 needed for Waldberg to die. He was never offered the opportunity to become part of the Double-Cross system, which means one of two things: either his arrest and detention were seen by members of the public, which meant that he was unsuitable to be part of the system, or that he was offered the opportunity to become part of it, but turned it down. I can only believe that the decision not to include him in the Double-Cross system was to do with his arrest, because if he had been offered the opportunity to become a double agent, one of the things that would have been clearly pointed out to him, were his limited options if he declined. He would have been told in no uncertain terms that if he did not agree to go against the *Abwehr*, he would face a trial under the Treachery Act, and what the outcome of that would have been. Being in possession of that information, there would have been no option for him but to acquiesce in what MI5 were asking him to do. At trial he would have never agreed to plead guilty as he would have clearly known the consequences of making such a decision.

All official MI5 and Home Office references to him were kept under the name of Waldberg and not Lassudry. By doing so, life was a lot less complicated, for staying with the name Waldberg and keeping him as a German national gave more credibility to their ultimate treatment of him. Had they referred to him as Lassudry, they would in essence have to admit the possibility that they had made a mistake. The letters which Waldberg/Lassundry wrote to his family and girlfriend were never sent, in part because of some of the content, but also because if MI5 had forwarded them on they would also be admitting that they believed his story that he was Lassundry and the reasons behind why he agreed to work for the *Abwehr* in the first place. They remained in MI5 files for many years before being deposited at the National Archives in 2005.

Meier, we know was seen by all of the customers who were in the Rising Sun pub in Lydd when he tried to purchase alcohol, which made him unsuitable for being offered the opportunity of being a double agent. Pons and van den Kieboom's arrests must have also been quite public affairs for them to have been treated the same as Meier.

Although attempts have always been made to legitimise and justify war, by attaching rules to it in an effort to make it less distasteful, it has to be remembered that war is nothing other than legalised murder. But the British in particular have always struggled with that concept, because 'it's not British' or 'that's not how we do things'. Well, as shocking as that concept might be to some, it should also be remembered that no country fights a war to come second. Being a runner-up means defeat and annihilation. What happened to Waldberg in particular, was always going to happen, because this wasn't about what was right or wrong, it was about winning the war, plain and simple. If MI5 felt that they had to take a certain course of action, no matter how distasteful it might have been, they did it for the right reasons and not out of any personal malice towards Waldberg/Lassundry. In war there are many casualties, and he was one of them, of that there is no doubt.

Besides Meir, Waldberg, Pons and van den Kieboom, fifteen other German spies who were sent to England by Germany's *Abwehr* during the Second World War, were captured, and prosecuted under the Treachery Act, found guilty and sentenced to death. In 1946, with the war over, the now redundant Treachery Act was suspended and fully removed from the statute books a few years later. It would be fair to say that MI5 did not enjoy the experience of the court hearings involving those they had charged under the Treachery Act, even though every one of them was carried out in camera, or in layman's terms, behind closed doors without the presence of any reporters. There were just too many people, windows and doors to cover. All MI5 could do was hope that somebody wasn't standing behind one of them, listening and observing what was been said.

The Double-Cross system had to be absolutely water-tight to have any chance of being the effective tool that it so badly needed to be. It wasn't until many years after the war that the real worth of MI5 and the part they had played in helping Britain and her allies win the Second World War, was fully appreciated. They did this by a number of methods, of which intelligence, espionage and counter espionage were the cornerstones. A big part of this was the Double-Cross system.

It wasn't just the court proceedings that gave MI5 cause for concern. Once the defendant had been found guilty, they then had to be transferred back to the prison where they were being held, which in most cases was Pentonville. There was a requirement that a notice of execution had to be displayed on the prison's main gates, for a period of twenty-four hours before the hanging took place. As if that wasn't enough for MI5 to have to concern themselves with, there was also a requirement for an inquest to take place into the death by hanging, which required a jury and a coroner to hear all the evidence as to the reasons behind the execution. The only time things were handled differently was if the defendant was a member of the armed forces of an enemy country, then they would face a court martial that was held at a military establishment. This meant inquest, no jury, no coroner, no press, and no need to place a notice on the gates of the barracks.

After the war, MI5 was confident enough to announce that every German agent sent to England by the *Abwehr*, was captured, and either executed or turned into a double agent, but they could never be one hundred per cent certain that was the case, although it would be safe to say that they captured most of them.

Chapter Two

Hermann Görtz

The story of Hermann Görtz is included here, despite the fact that he was not a German spy who was caught in Britain during the Second World War. He was convicted of 'spying' in England in 1936 for which he served a four-year prison sentence, an offence for which, had it taken place during the Second World War, he would have been executed. The other reason for including his story is that he was parachuted into Ireland in 1940 by the *Abwehr* to be their liaison officer with the IRA. One of the things he was asked to look at was the viability of a joint IRA/German invasion of Northern Ireland should Germany succeed in invading and capturing Great Britain. He was a very interesting character.

During the Second World War, Hermann Görtz was a German spy working for the *Abwehr*. Born in Lübeck, in northern Germany on 15 November 1890, he served during the First World War, initially as an infantryman on the Eastern Front, where he was wounded whilst fighting against Russian forces. Sometime after he had recovered from his wounds, he decided that he wanted to become a pilot in the German Air Force. After finishing his basic training, he became a reconnaissance pilot, where he served alongside Hermann Goering, flying across enemy lines to try and locate the build-up of enemy troops.

It wasn't long before his skills as an interrogator of captured enemy pilots and air crews came to notice. He displayed a natural talent for it and became quite accomplished at getting prisoners to talk. Because of this he was promoted to the rank of captain and became an interrogations officer.

After the war, Görtz returned to civilian life and became a law student, a subject that he was sufficiently good at to earn a doctorate in international law. During this time, he married Ellen Aschenborn, the daughter of German Admiral z.D. Aschenborn, who in 1914, just after the start of the war, had been in charge of the *Freiwilliges Motorboot Korps*.

Görtz's involvement in international law saw him travelling to many countries. It was on one such trip to Ireland in 1927 to research the relationship between Ireland and the United Kingdom from a legal perspective that he fell in love with the country. He saw parallels between what was happening politically in Ireland in her relationship with the United Kingdom under the auspices of the Anglo-Irish Treaty, in the same way that Germany had suffered under the Treaty of Versailles, to which the United Kingdom was a signatory.

On 29 August 1935 Hermann Görtz, arrived in England with a German woman by the name of Marianne Emig, who was apparently his secretary. For the first few weeks they spent time travelling round Suffolk, taking in the picturesque countryside. From there they travelled to Broadstairs in Kent, where they rented a house for six weeks, which wasn't far from the RAF base at Manston. During their time there they became acquainted with a young airman who was stationed at the base, Kenneth Lewis. How that friendship came about is unclear, but it was possibly whilst drinking at one of the local pubs. The friendship flourished sufficiently for Emig to be able to ask Lewis to take photographs of the air base along with the aircraft that flew out of it, but without providing any reason for why she wanted them. She told him that she wanted photographs of RAF aircraft and aerial photographs of both RAF Manston and RAF Lee-on-Solent, and that she would pay for films and their development.

As the six-week rental of the property in Broadstairs came to an end, Görtz and Emig returned to Germany for a short time. After just a few days in Germany, he sent Mrs Florence Johnson, the owner of the property he was renting, a telegram from Germany dated 24 October 1935, saying he was away for a few days and would she be kind enough to keep an eye on his motorcycle for him. When she checked on the bungalow, she discovered that his motorcycle had been taken from the property. She reported this to the local police, who began investigating the matter. Whilst making their enquiries at the property in Broadstairs, police officers discovered paperwork and drawings of RAF Manston that were directly connected to Görtz. They also found a part-written undated letter to his wife in which he referred to the fact that he wished to place himself at the disposal of the secret service and to show them they had made a mistake in refusing him. There was also a copy of an application form regarding employment with the German Intelligence Service and also a cypher indicator.

Mrs Johnson had also found a camera in his motorcycle overalls. The combination of these findings made him a marked man. Three weeks later on 8 November, this time travelling unaccompanied, the police became aware that he had returned to England via the Port of Harwich on the Essex coast, and he was arrested. Amongst items he had in his possession were three letters sent by Kenneth Lewis and photographs of aircraft he had taken and sent to Emig.

Görtz was charged with 'spying' under the Official Secrets Act and appeared at the Central Criminal Courts at the Old Bailey in the City of London in March 1936. The trial was front page news in both England and Germany, despite Görtz pleading not guilty. One of those called to give evidence at the trial was Aircraftman Kenneth Lewis. He told the court that he was stationed at RAF Lee-on-Solent. He remembered being on leave when his motorcycle broke down at Crow Hill, and suddenly out of nowhere Miss Emig appeared and asked if she could help. For the remaining week of his leave, they met up every day. One of these occasions was at the bungalow in Broadstairs where they had tea when Dr Görtz was also present. Lewis was taken by surprise at just how much the pair of them seemed to know about the Royal Air Force. Miss Emig told him that she had flown gliders back home in Germany, and she even asked him to come and spend a holiday there. When he said that he would not be able to afford such a trip, she told him that she would help him financially.

He had written to Miss Emig at addresses she had given him in Hamburg and Berlin and said that he had received two letters and two postcards from her, which he had destroyed after reading them as she had requested him to do so. Mr Parham, questioning Lewis, produced three letters which Lewis said he had written to Emig. Mr Parham then informed Lewis that the three letters he had sent to Emig had been found amongst the possessions of Dr Görtz when he had been arrested at Harwich, and the letters contained photographs of RAF aircraft.

Lewis said that he had also sent Emig newspaper cuttings and a semi-aerial view of the Lee-on-Solent RAF base that had no military value. He agreed that he had sent them at her request but stated that they contained no secret information, and those that he sent her could be obtained from most shops. He also said that he was asked to label the envelopes of the letters he sent her with the RAF crest.

Detective Sergeant Allen of Kent Constabulary told the court that when he searched Dr Görtz and his baggage, he discovered a number of documents. One was a newspaper cutting about Wing Commander Smith of the RAF. There was a letter from Doctor Heinrich Rohl, a diary and notebook and a page from the *Air Pilot* that related to Hornchurch.

Detective Sergeant Ivor T. Williams said that he had a strange conversation with Görtz whilst acting as a custody sergeant. He had told the sergeant that he had visited England many times up until 1931 whilst working for Siemens as their lawyer. He also said that he had been a pilot during the First World War, and then added that he did some private flying with the Nazi flying club in Hamburg.

The evidence against Görtz weighed heavy; he was found guilty and sentenced to four years imprisonment, which he served at Maidstone Prison in Kent. His defence during the case had been that the sketches and documentation that had been found, were part of his research for a book he intended to write about the Royal Air Force. He had no previous experience of writing any kind of book, let alone one that was aimed at a foreign audience. His secretary, Marianne Emig, did not help his cause when she refused to return to England to give evidence on his behalf at the trial. Her stance wasn't wholly unreasonable as she was probably in fear of being arrested herself and charged with similar offences. Görtz was released from prison one month short of having served three years in prison, and was immediately deported to Germany, deemed to be an undesirable alien.

The following are newspaper reports about Görtz and his court appearances in 1935 and 1936. The first article is taken from the front page of the *Staffordshire Sentinel*, dated Tuesday, 19 November 1935.

It was learned today that Doctor Hermann Görtz, a German, was arrested recently in England, and charged under the Official Secrets Act.

He has been remanded by a magistrate and will appear before the courts in the normal way. It has not yet been officially disclosed where Dr Görtz was arrested, or at which court he will appear. It is understood however, that Dr Görtz was arrested at Harwich, on behalf of the Kent Police, and taken to a Kentish seaside resort.

The Deputy Clerk to the Margate Magistrates, when asked today whether a Dr Hermann Görtz had appeared before a magistrate or magistrates in that court, said: 'I will not deny that. You may take it from me that the next trial will be in camera.'

Later it was learned that Dr Görtz appeared before a magistrate of the Cinque Ports Petty Sessions, who sat privately in a committee room at the same place yesterday. The proceedings lasted only a few minutes. He was brought to the town in a Metropolitan Police van, and left Margate in the same van at about 2.15pm yesterday.

Dr Görtz is now in Brixton Prison, and it is expected that he will appear in court at Margate on Thursday or Friday, it being understood that the charge has reference to Manston Aerodrome, which is near Broadstairs. It is expected that the case will then be inquired into, but the proceedings will be in camera.

From inquiries in London it is learned that for ten days Scotland Yard officers have been associated with the Kent Constabulary in investigations in the Margate and Broadstairs area.

An official of the German Embassy said today he received this morning from Doctor Hermann Görtz a letter asking the Embassy to send him a list of German speaking solicitors. 'Until I had read the letter,' said the official, 'I had never heard of Doctor Görtz. We get letters quite frequently from Germans, asking us to let them have the names of German speaking solicitors, and therefore I took no more notice of this letter than of the others.

The letter was written from Brixton prison. Doctor Görtz said in it that he was in gaol on a serious charge, but he did not say what the charge was. In accordance with our usual practice, we are sending to him list of German speaking solicitors, and that is all we know about the matter.'

Tuesday, 26 November 1935, saw an article appear in the *Portsmouth Evening News* in relation to Görtz case:

When the case against Hermann Görtz, a German doctor and lawyer, who is charged under the Official Secrets Act, was opened in public at Margate today, allegations were made that he and a young woman, described as his niece, became friendly with a young aircraftsman from Manston aerodrome.

Görtz had previously been remanded before a private sitting of the magistrate. Mr H.J. Parham, for the Director of Public Prosecutions, today stated that only Air Ministry and other technical witnesses would be heard in private.

The young woman, said Mr Parham, was named Marianne Emig, and was said to be Görtz's niece. The aircraftman visited them at their bungalow at Broadstairs, and Miss Emig said to him, 'You must remember that in the next war England and Germany will be on the same side.'

Miss Emig and the young airman arranged to write to one another. She asked him to let her have photographs of RAF machines and also invited him to Germany. Mr Parham described how Görtz and Miss Emig had left for German. Police visited his bungalow and found a sketch of Manston aerodrome and other documents. On his return to this country a large number of articles were found on Dr Görtz which, according to Mr Parham, showed that he had been assiduously collecting whatever information he could relating to the Royal Air Force.

Mr Parham said that in his statement Dr Görtz made the points that he was collecting material for a novel and for an essay on the enlargement of the British Air Force, that what he did he did openly, and that he had no intention of infringing the law.

The article also included a statement from the War Office which outlined the charges against Görtz:

> That at the parish of Broadstairs and St Peter's between September 18 and October 23, 1935, he acted in contravention of Section 1 (B) of the Official Secrets Act, 1911, as amended by the Official Secrets Act 1920.
>
> That between September 18 and October 24, 1935, at Broadstairs, he conspired with another person, not in custody, to commit offences against the Official Secrets Act 1911 and 1920. Dr Görtz, who holds both medical and law degrees, studied surgery in Edinburgh before the war. The War Office statement explained that Dr Görtz was arrested at Harwich on November 8 and was charged before the magistrates at Broadstairs under the provisions of the Official Secrets Act the following day, when he was remanded in custody.
>
> He again appeared before the magistrates at a special private sitting of the Cinque Ports Petty Sessions at the Town Hall Margate, on Tuesday November 12, when evidence of arrest only was given, and he was remanded in custody until today.
>
> When Dr Görtz arrived at Margate in a Police van from Brixton prison, escorted by four warders, he covered his face with a handkerchief and passed into the Police station. Tall and rather pale, Dr Görtz was wearing a trilby hat and fawn mackintosh, and his barrister, was a Mr Alexander Cairns.
>
> Hermann Görtz was called, and a tall, very upright figure stepped into the dock. His fair hair was immaculately brushed, and he wore a smart double-breasted suit, khaki shirt, and red tie. He frowned in a puzzled way as if he had difficulty in following the proceedings in English.

Mr Parham then told the court that Hermann Görtz, a German subject landed at Harwich on 29 August 1935, and described himself as a lawyer and novelist, who had come to study export law cases at Cambridge. Despite the fact that he was supposedly writing a book on the enlargement of the Royal Air Force so that he could pay off his creditors, he could still finance his trip to England; not just the cost of the crossing, but the rent for the cottage in Broadstairs, as well as money for food and other incidentals. His diary that he had with him at the time of his arrest, showed no record of him having ever visited Cambridge. In fact, most of his time was spent in and around Mildenhall, Suffolk, which was home to a large Royal Air Force base. On 11 September 1935, he arrived in Broadstairs with Marianne Emig, and called at an estate agent and rented a bungalow in Stanley Road, Broadstairs.

Friday, 7 February 1936 saw an article about the trial appear in *The Scotsman* newspaper, reporting its postponement.

The trial of Dr Hermann Görtz, the 44-year-old German lawyer, committed from Margate on charges of espionage, was postponed at the Old Bailey, London, yesterday until next sessions. Görtz is accused of conspiring with Marianne Emig to commit offences under the Official Secrets Act. He is charged with making a sketch plan or note of Manston Royal Air Force Station, which was calculated to be or might be, or was intended to be, directly or indirectly, useful to an enemy.

Mr Alexander Cairns, defending, applied for the trial not to be taken until next sessions. There were, he said, two reasons for the application. One was that there was a great deal of research work being undertaken in Germany. The defence had the depositions at Christmas, but did not finish their work until nearly the middle of January. They were now engaged in intensive research work in Germany tracing the origin of certain documents which were put in.

The other thing was the matter of funds, so that Mr Görtz should be adequately represented. The defence was collecting from the relatives of the accused a certain amount, but permission had to be obtained by the German government to send money out of the country.

Mr L.A. Byrne, for the director of Public Prosecutions, said that the case was completed on November 25, but Dr Görtz was not then committed, in order to give him the benefit of an adjournment over the session. The case was adjourned until December 3, when he was formally committed for trial. When he came before the Central Criminal Court an application was made for a postponement of the trial, and this was consented to. The application then was on the same grounds.

The Judge said; 'I cannot see that there is any ground for further adjournment. It is not in the interests of justice to adjourn a case too long. Witnesses may die or their memories may be less accurate. These matters should be disposed of while the facts are reasonably fresh in the minds of witnesses.'

Mr Cairns responded: 'One thing I have to do is bring over certain official witnesses from the Courts in Hamburg. It takes some time to get them permission to have leave from the country.

One thing is a cipher. Dr Görtz is a lawyer in Hamburg, and we can show how that cipher came into his possession in connection with legal proceedings in Germany. That has taken some time to find out, and we have to get certain officials who can prove the origin of that cipher.'

The Judge then agreed that he would postpone the hearing until the next sessions, but only on that ground.

Despite having previously been turned down by the German Air Ministry prior to going to England, Görtz was employed by the *Abwehr* soon after his return and went on to reach the rank of major. In May 1940 the *Abwehr* in Berlin sanctioned and planned a spying mission, code named Operation Mainau, which involved parachuting one of its agents into Ireland, to meet up with a senior and respected member of the Irish Republican Army, Seamus 'Jim' O'Donovan, who was one of their explosives experts. He was the author of the IRA's S-Plan, which was a bombing campaign on nominated targets in England. The *Abwehr* agent involved was Hermann Görtz.

O'Donovan was well known to the *Abwehr*, and a man whom they trusted. He had made three visits to Germany in the months immediately prior to the outbreak of the war. On the first meeting in Hamburg on 26 February 1939, he conducted business on behalf of the IRA for firearms and radio equipment, and on 26 April the same year, he negotiated a second firearms deal between the *Abwehr* and the IRA, which saw the agreed weapons delivered to Dublin via France.

Görtz's journey to Ireland began from Fritzlar airfield in Germany at 9pm on the evening of 4 May 1940, on board a Heinkel He 111 medium bomber aircraft. The weather that night was not good, but needs must. His actions that night were certainly brave, as he exited the aircraft at an altitude of just 1,500 metres, which left absolutely no margin for error. It wouldn't have been an easy jump to make in daylight, so to undertake it during the hours of darkness in inclement weather certainly took some nerves. By the time he had landed he discovered he had lost his all-important radio and his lifeline with Germany. He also lost his shovel which is what he was going to use to bury his parachute.

Görtz successfully parachuted into Ireland, landing at Ballivor in County Meath. His job was to be the liaison officer between the German authorities and the IRA. This link was more about Germany's planning for the future, and her intended invasion and occupation of Great Britain which, of course, never materialised.

His mission had four points to it. He was to establish a secure communications link between Ireland and Germany; consult with the IRA on the prospect of a reconciliation between them and the Irish state; direct the military activities of the IRA towards British military targets, rather than civilian ones, especially any and all naval installations, and to report any incidental items of military importance.

After having landed safely, he unclipped his parachute and removed his flying suit to reveal a pristine Luftwaffe dress uniform. Remarkably Görtz made no attempt to hide his uniform and set off on foot towards his intended destination of Laragh, in County Wicklow, a distance of some eighty miles. Even more remarkable was the fact that on the way there he stopped off at the Garda Barracks in County Wicklow, still dressed in his German military uniform, asking for directions to where he was going, which he was given. Amazingly, he was not detained or questioned about who he was or what he was doing walking around Ireland in a German uniform. He arrived safely in Laragh on 9 May 1940 where he met up with his host Mrs Stuart. Later that evening Görtz was collected by Seamus O'Donovan of the IRA, who took him to his own home, 'Florenceville', which was situated in Shankill Killiney, County Dublin. Just two days later on 11 May, Görtz was taken by O'Donovan and two other men to the home of another IRA member in Rathmines, J.J. O'Neil, where he remained until 19 May. Whilst there Görtz handed over $165,000 in American dollars.

During his time in Ireland he was often on the move, in an effort to stay out of the clutches of the Irish authorities, who, it must be said, could have saved themselves a great deal of time and trouble, if they had arrested him when he asked for directions in County Wicklow.

Stephen Carroll Held was a member of the IRA in Dublin and also of German descent. That connection alone made Held an obvious person of interest for the Garda to want to speak to in relation to trying to locate Görtz. In May 1940 Held's home at Blackheath Park in Dublin was raided by the Garda. The result of the raid was better than they could have ever hoped for. They found a parachute, a number of documents that included information about military targets in Ireland, such as airfields, military barracks and harbours, and details of a planned joint IRA and Nazi operation for the invasion of Northern Ireland, known as Plan Kathleen. Amongst the illicit find were Görtz's military medals from his service in the First World War.

Neither Held nor Görtz were at home at the time of the raid and remained at large. It would be another eighteen months before Görtz would be captured at an IRA safehouse in Dublin. In November 1940 an IRA member visited a house in Dublin. It is not clear whether it was the house or the IRA member who was being watched, but when the Garda pounced on the address it turned out to be where Görtz was hiding and, along with the IRA member, he was arrested.

The *Abwehr* war diary for the date of 25 May 1940 recorded the following entry:

> According to a wireless report of the Stefani Agency (Italian news agency) and enemy broadcasts, 'Operation Mainau' has been unsuccessful. According to them 'Gilka' appears to have reached his destination. The transmitter [the Abwehr did not know Görtz had lost it], some items of equipment and the money which he took with him were apparently seized in the house of an Irish agent, through the latter's stupidity. Unfortunately, this Irishman also had in his possession plans for a rebellion which had no connection with 'Operation Mainau'. There is no information as to Gilka's whereabouts. Even if he is not arrested in the near future, his further activity is rendered impossible in consequence of the discovery of the transmitter and the money. If he should eventually be arrested, Gilka is in a very difficult position in consequence of his equipment being found in the same place as the IRA plans. In consequence of the failure of 'Operation Mainau' proposals for the parachuting of further agents are for the future to be disregarded.

'Gilka' was the *Abwehr*'s code name for Görtz. He later said of his time in Ireland:

> I lived among people of my choice and never again under the protection of the IRA. I personally chose all the houses in which I hid, or they were chosen for me by my friends. I carefully avoided any hide-out which had anything to do with the IRA. When I heard in one house that it had formerly been an IRA meeting place, I left it the same night. I realised that an agreement between the Irish government and the IRA was completely inopportune. The action against Held ruled out all hopes of bringing the IRA into association with the government.

The Held episode had, however, a good side to it: I shook off the unwanted IRA protection. For the future, I was able to work with people whom I chose myself.

Ireland was a neutral nation during the Second World War, and other than having entered the country illegally, Görtz hadn't, as far as the authorities knew, actually committed any criminal offences. Yes, they had found documents about possible future operations against both Ireland and Northern Ireland, but there was no direct evidence to prove that any or all of the recovered documents actually had anything to do with Görtz. Although he faced no criminal charges, he was interned by the Irish authorities as he was unarguably a member of the German military. He was initially held at Mountjoy Prison in Dublin, before being transferred to Custume Barracks in Athlone, where he remained until August 1946 when he was finally released and went to live in the Glenageary district of Dublin.

Sometime in early 1947, Görtz was served with a deportation order by the Minister for Justice, informing him that he was being sent back to Germany. Why or how this order came about is unclear, as he had not committed any offence subsequent to his release from internment, and by all accounts had been a model citizen. Despite his attempts at appealing this decision, he failed.

He arrived at the Aliens Office at Dublin Castle on the morning of Friday, 23 May 1947, to be informed that he was being deported to Germany the following day. Despite being told that the Irish government had specifically requested that he must not be handed over to the Russians, Görtz committed suicide.

The following report in relation to Görtz appeared in the *Irish Times* newspaper on Saturday, 24 May 1947.

He stared disbelievingly at the detective officers. Then suddenly, he took his hand from his trouser pocket, swiftly removed his pipe from between his lips, and slipped a small glass phial into his mouth. One of the police officers sprang at

Goertz as he crunched the glass with his teeth. The officer got his hands around Goertz's neck but failed to prevent most of the poison – believed to be prussic acid, from passing down his throat. Within a few seconds, Görtz collapsed. He was driven to Mercer's Hospital in the city, and died there shortly after his arrival.

Görtz was buried in a Dublin cemetery just three days after his death, and in 1974 his remains were exhumed and transferred to the German Military Cemetery at Glencree in County Wicklow. There is no record of MI5 or anybody from the Home Office having ever requested to interview Görtz in relation to what he knew of plans by Germany to invade mainland Britain and Northern Ireland.

Chapter Three
Josef Jakobs

Joseph Jacobs holds the distinction of being the last person to be executed at the Tower of London on 15 August 1941, when he was shot by firing squad in the Tower's miniature rifle range. All other German spies who were captured and executed during the Second World War, were hanged. The reason Jakobs was shot by firing squad was because he was captured as an enemy combatant.

Although born in Luxembourg, he was a German citizen having served in the 4th Foot Guards, an infantry regiment of the Royal Prussian Army during the First World War, which was disbanded in June 1919.

In June 1940, aged 42, Jakobs was drafted into the German Army and given the rank he had finished on at the end of the First World War, that of *Leutnant*. During the interwar years he hadn't exactly conducted himself as might have been expected of an officer and a gentleman. He spent some four years in prison in Switzerland for fraud, between 1934 and 1937, when he became involved in selling fake gold. Once this indiscretion had been discovered by the German military authorities, he had no option but to resign his commission in disgrace. But as fit and able men were at a premium during the war, he was not dismissed from the *Wehrmacht*, but demoted to the rank of *Feldwebel* which was a non-commissioned officer rank, similar to that of a sergeant. The demotion also came with a not so popular posting to the *Meteorogischen Dienst* or in English, the meteorological service.

It is not clear how the move came about, but it wasn't long before he was working for the *Abwehr*, the German Army's intelligence service. After having completed his 'spy' training, his masters decided that he was ready to be sent on his first mission, so on the evening of 31 January 1941, he was flown from Schiphol airport in Holland, across the English Channel, to carry out his spying mission in England. As he flew over the town of

Ramsey in the heart of the Huntingdonshire countryside on a cold winter's night, he parachuted out of his aircraft. There is an element of confusion about what happened next, but one thing is for sure: after he landed he was immediately aware that he had broken his ankle. The confusion comes from whether he broke the ankle by catching it on the side of the aircraft when he parachuted, or by landing awkwardly when he hit the ground. Either way, it was an unfortunate accident that would eventually cost him his life.

He landed in a snow-covered potato field that was part of Dove House Farm in Ramsey, very close to the RAF airbase at Upwood. Despite his best efforts he couldn't even get up off the ground, let alone walk anywhere. He spent a cold night, wrapped in his parachute to try and keep himself warm. By the morning, realising that his situation was somewhat limited, he took out his revolver and fired it into the air to attract attention. Two farm workers, Charles Baldock and Harry Coulson, heard the gunshots and went to investigate. Unsure as to who the man they had discovered was, they called one of their fellow workers, Harry Godfrey, who was also a member of the local Ramsey Home Guard.

A newspaper report of the time detailed Josef Jakobs' arrest:

JOSEF JACOBS SPY IN SPATS CAUGHT BY H.G.

Josef Jacobs was a dandy. He landed here, by parachute in a grey-striped suit, grey overcoat, brown trilby hat and spats. Yesterday he was shot in the Tower of London as a spy, captured by Home Guard Lance Corporal Harry Godfrey a 39-year-old tractor driver somewhere in England.

'Josef Jacobs' was the name on the British identity card and ration book he carried when he dropped into a potato field in the Home Counties during a snowstorm. He hoped to set up his own little weather station on British soil, to give the Luftwaffe daily reports for a 'target for tonight'. But Goering never received a single dot or dash.

Jacobs hid for 12 hours in the lonely field, his parachute wrapped closely around him through the wild night, a fitting night for a meteorologist. He was seen in the morning by two agricultural labourers, Charlie Baldock and Harry Coulson. His adventures ended in a drive to the police station on a farm cart.

'Me flying – me bale out 100 metres', said the spy to Home Guard Harry Godfrey who took him prisoner. Said Harry Godfrey, number four recruit to his local platoon: 'Oh, yes? Well, where the blazes is your plane?' Mr Jacobs decided to answer no further questions.

Lance Corporal Godfrey had been starting up a chaff-cutter on the farm when Harry Coulson dashed into the yard and shouted 'Harry, we've seen a German here, I reckon it's a spy. Phone the police.'

Harry in shirt, knee breeches and puttees waded through the mud and slush to the spot where Jacobs was hiding. 'He had been smoking all night. There were about 30 cigarette ends lying all around him,' he said. 'He tried to light another one but the petrol in his lighter had run out. He threw his revolver towards Baldock as they ran up to him. He had managed to throw away a little steel shovel like kiddies use at the seaside with which he had buried his radio set. But I kicked against something hard and discovered a fibre suitcase with a five-valve radio set inside, a few inches under the soil. There was a coil of insulated aerial as well.

In his tin hat were two half-pound blocks of chocolate. In his pockets were a packet of black bread sandwiches, brandy, an identity card, and a ration book. I did not notice whether any coupons had been used. He wore a flying suit over his suit and looked very smart but for his shoes. They were down at heel and badly worn.

A dark-haired man, he seemed to be a poor specimen physically, He was about 5ft 6ins in height and weighed only 9st, and apparently he was very hungry. His hair had a grey tinge by the time his court-martial was held.'

Jacobs carried two wads of £1 notes in his breast pockets, they totalled nearly £500. 'Me not in war – me from Luxemburg made to come,' was his defence. He also said he had a wife and three children. But an official statement issued after his execution yesterday described him as a German born in Luxemburg on 30 June 1898, a non-commissioned officer in the German Army attached to the Meteorological Service. It added that he was convicted under the Treachery Act after trial by General Court Martial held on August 4 and 5 in camera. A barrister, at present serving in the forces, as well as an interpreter were put at his disposal for his defence.

This execution was the first carried out by firing squad of the war at the Tower.

As was reported in the newspaper article, he was still wearing his flying suit and helmet over his civilian clothes. He had two bundles of £1 bank notes, each of £250 concealed in his jacket pockets. He was also in possession of forged identity papers, food rations and a radio transmitter. In another pocket he had a photograph that he claimed was of his lover, Clara Bauerie, a German actress and cabaret singer, who before the war had worked in theatre in the West Midlands and could speak perfect English in a Birmingham accent. He informed the British authorities that she was also a spy, and that the plan was for her to join him in England once he had confirmed that he had arrived safely, but he had been arrested before being able to make any such contact.

Initially Jakobs was taken to the local police station at Ramsey. It is interesting to note at this point that he wasn't taken to hospital, either civilian or military, but instead he was transferred to Cannon Row Police Station in London, where he was interviewed by Major T.A. Robertson from MI5. It was only later that day when he was transferred to Brixton Prison to be held overnight, that he received medical attention to his ankle in the prison's infirmary. The following morning he was transferred to Camp 020 at Latchmere House, in South London, which was a British interrogation centre for captured German agents during the Second World War. It was the man in charge, Lieutenant Colonel Robin 'Tin Eye' Stephens, who re-interviewed Jakobs after his arrival. Later that day Jakobs was transferred to Dulwich Hospital, where he remained for the following two months, whilst recovering from his broken ankle.

Jakobs faced a court martial that took place over two days on 4 and 5 August 1941, at the Duke of York's headquarters in Chelsea. The proceedings were held in private for reasons of national security, as it transpired that British Military Intelligence, MI5, were aware that Jakobs was to arrive in England. They had been informed of his arrival by Arthur Owens, a Welsh Nationalist and a double agent. This was part of the highly classified intelligence operation, known as the Double-Cross System, which could not be made public at the time.

In total, eight witnesses gave evidence against Jakobs which resulted in his being found guilty under the Treachery Act and sentenced to death.

His execution was carried out on 15 August 1941 at the Tower of London, by means of an eight-man firing squad from the Tower's holding battalion of the Scots Guards. Each of the eight-man detachment took aim with their .303 Lee Enfield rifles, aiming directly at Jakobs' heart. At precisely 7.12am, Lieutenant Colonel C.R. Gerard, the Deputy Provost Marshal for London, lowered his hand and all eight men fired in unison. Five bullets struck Jakobs in and around the area of his heart, killing him instantly, the other three bullets fired were blanks, meaning that none of the men could ever know which of their bullets were live, or who had actually killed Jakobs. The reason behind this was the belief that soldiers, in such circumstances, felt uncomfortable about shooting an unarmed enemy who had no means of defending himself.

After the execution, Jakobs was pronounced dead by the attending doctor, and his body placed in a wooden casket. He was taken directly to St Mary's Catholic Cemetery, at Kensal Green, London, where he was buried in an unmarked grave.

In 2019 Jakobs granddaughter, Giselle Jakobs, wrote and published a book about him, entitled, *The Spy in the Tower – The untold story of Josef Jacobs, the last person to be executed in the Tower of London.*

Chapter Four

The Double-Cross System

During the Second World War, MI5 came up with a counter espionage operation that was known as the Double-Cross system, or the XX System. It was so entitled because it was the Twenty Committee, under the chairmanship of John Cecil Masterman, that oversaw the operations of MI5, and the number twenty in Roman numerals is 'XX' or double cross.

John Cecil Masterman was born in Kingston-upon-Thames, in Surrey. His education saw him read modern history at Worcester College, Oxford. Unfortunately for him, when the First World War began he was working in Germany as a lecturer at the University of Freiburg. This resulted in his spending the entire war years interned as an enemy alien at the Ruhleben Internment camp, some six miles west of Berlin. Not one to waste an opportunity, he spent that time learning German and becoming very proficient at it, an attribute that would be extremely useful to him during the Second World War. After his release from captivity in 1918, he returned to England and took up a position as a tutor at Christ Church, Oxford, where he taught Modern History. He was also a noted sportsman, who in 1931 was part of the squad who toured Canada with the Marylebone Cricket Club (MCC)

At the outbreak of the Second World War, Masterman was drafted into the Intelligence Corps and, after the evacuation of British, French and Belgian troops at Dunkirk, he was the person tasked with producing a report on the successful operation. Soon afterwards he became a civilian assistant within MI5, and as is well documented, he became chairman of the organization's Twenty Committee which, besides other things, oversaw the operations that were part of the Double-Cross system.

It was the job of those working in Section B1(a) of MI5 to locate German agents, convince them to become double agents, and then provide them with the information to feed back to their *Abwehr* masters in Germany. The man in charge of that section, and the person who was actually responsible for its formation was, Lieutenant Colonel T.A. Robertson. Both Masterman and Robertson were awarded the Order of the British Empire in June 1943, as well as the Yugoslav Crown in November 1945.

Thomas Argyll Robertson was born in Scotland in 1909. Part of the disinformation that Robertson had his double agents deliver to the German intelligence services played an important role in convincing the enemy that the Allied invasions that took place at Sicily in 1943 and on the beaches of Normandy on 6 June 1944, were not the actual locations where they were going to take place. It is fair to say that MI5's Double-Cross system of disinformation against the German intelligence services, worked better than they could ever have hoped for.

In simple terms, Nazi agents of the *Abwehr*, Germany's version of MI5, were either captured, or handed themselves in on their arrival in Britain, and were then used by MI5 to send back either low level information or disinformation to their handlers in Germany. The disinformation surrounding the invasion of Sicily in 1943, was given the operational name of 'Mincemeat'. Although the operation was one entirely of deception it did not directly involve the use of a double agent providing the German Intelligence Service with any kind of information.

The man who was actually responsible for making the operation work was a tramp, Glyndwr Michael, but he died as Captain/Acting Major William Martin. Whilst slumming it in an abandoned warehouse in Kings Cross, London, Welshman Glyndwr Michael died as a result of eating rat poison containing phosphorus which had been smeared on crusts of bread intended for rats. When he was discovered he was still alive and was taken to the nearby St Pancras Hospital, where he died two days later. He was 34 years of age.

It had been very difficult for MI5 to obtain a suitable body. Having someone who had no living relatives meant there would not be anybody turning up to claim his body. The authorities then obtained his body, dressed him up in the military uniform of an officer of the Royal Marines and placed identity documents on his body in the name of William Martin.

On 30 April 1943, the Royal Naval submarine HMS *Seraph* was in the seas off Huelva on the Spanish Atlantic coast, when it broke the surface.

Martin's body, which had been preserved in ice, was brought up on deck and the submarine's commanding officer, Lieutenant Norman Jewell, read a prayer from the Bible before the body was slipped into the water. Attached to his right wrist was a locked attaché case which supposedly contained secret documentation from one British general to another stating that the Allies were planning to invade Greece and Sardinia, with Sicily simply being a decoy target to throw the Germans off the scent. The hope was that Martin's body would wash up on the Spanish coastline somewhere in the area of Huelva, where it was known that Germany had spies.

Martin's body was spotted by a local fisherman who recovered his body out at sea and brought it back to shore where it was buried with full military honours in Huelva. The inscription on the headstone of his grave, read as follows.

William Martin, born 29 March 1907, died 24 April 1943, beloved son of John Glyndwyr Martin and the late Antonia Martin of Cardiff, Wales, Dulce et Decorum est pro Patria Mori, RIP.

The translation of the Latin phrase is, 'It is sweet and fitting to die for one's country.'

The operation had gone ahead with the knowledge and approval of both General Dwight D. Eisenhower, the Allied military commander in the Mediterranean, and the British Prime Minister, Winston Churchill. Even though Spain was a neutral country in the war, the Spanish government shared copies of the documents in the attaché case chained to Martin's wrist, with *Abwehr* agents. When the Spanish government gave the documents back to the British, they carried out tests on them which confirmed they had been read, and the subsequent intercept of German radio messages showed they believed the content of the documents they had read from Martin's attaché case. Germany did not send any reinforcements to Sicily, but instead sent them to Greece and Sardinia. Even during the actual invasion of Sicily, still the Germans did not send any reinforcements, believing that the fighting there was just a ruse to deter them from sending reinforcements to Greece and Sardinia.

Dropping the body of Glyndwyr Martin off the Spanish coast was a master stroke of subterfuge. It greatly reduced the number of anticipated Allied casualties, and Sicily was liberated much sooner than had been expected.

It was as recently as 1998 that the British Government revealed the true identity of Captain Williams, although it had been known for many years. On Tuesday, 10 March 1953, a short article appeared in the *Western Mail* newspaper, which spoke of a book that had been written by Ewen E.S. Montague, entitled *The Man Who Never Was*. The article read as follows:

> If the Germans had detected a spelling error in a Welsh name, an audacious and successful piece of bluff perpetrated by the Allies in World War II might have been ruined. The story of the exploit is related by the Hon. Ewen E.S. Montague in his book, *The Man Who Never Was*. The name selected for 'The Man Who Never Was', was William Martin and he was the son of John Glyndwr Martin, of Cardiff, according to the inscription on his tombstone. In Wales we write 'Glyndwr' and one wonders how the Germans would have reacted if they had discovered even this small error in the elaborate structure built to deceive them.

Lieutenant Commander Ewen E.S. Montague, who served in the Naval Intelligence Division of the British Admiralty during the Second World War, was the person, along with Squadron Leader Charles Cholmondeley of the Royal Air Force Volunteer Reserve, who came up with the idea of Operation Mincemeat, which is how Glyndwr Martin became the man who never was.

The Double-Cross system was so top-secret that the first book on the subject, John Masterman's *The Double-Cross System in the War of 1939–45*, was only published in 1972. Masterman had wanted to publish a book on the subject but was refused permission to do so by the British intelligence establishment. Both the head of MI5, Roger Hollis, and the British Prime Minister Alec Douglas-Home had repeatedly refused to authorize publication. His first attempt to get the work published had been in 1958. When he was turned down again in 1970, he decided to have the book published outside the UK, where he felt the Official Secrets Act would not hold any sway. In the end he chose Yale University Press as his publisher. Although he was initially threatened by the British establishment with prosecution if he published the work, they eventually bowed to the inevitable and allowed Masterman's book to be published. I believe there was a realisation by the establishment that the story about the Double Cross system would come out sooner than later, so who better to write that story than the chairman of the Twenty Committee, John Masterman.

The system didn't begin as what it eventually became. It was initially in place for counter-espionage purposes, to capture enemy agents who had come to Britain to either obtain information and documents useful to their country, or to carry out acts of sabotage or murder. It was only as time went on that the idea to use the system and the captured enemy agents to deceive their masters back in Germany was undertaken. The agents were sent by the German intelligence services, *Abwehr* and *Sicherheitsdienst*. We will look at both agencies in more detail elsewhere in the book, but the latter of the two, also referred to by the initials SD, was the intelligence agency of the SS and the Nazi Party. Originating in 1931, the *Sicherheitsdienst* was the first Nazi intelligence organization to be established.

Some of the agents who arrived in Britain weren't actually agents at all. They had simply tricked the Germans into making them believe that they would spy for them, when in essence it was just a way of being able to reach England. They were known as false agents. The Germans used different methods to infiltrate their spies into the country. Some would be parachuted in, whilst others would arrive by submarine and row into shore. Some would arrive by boat pretending to be refugees, which was the preferred method and certainly the less-riskier option. The false agents still had to persuade the British authorities on their arrival that they were not German agents. It was a good story to come up with, especially if an individual was actually a German spy and was simply trying to hoodwink the British authorities into believing they were not.

Two of the so-called false agents were Nathalie Sergueiew, who was born in St Petersburg, Russia in 1912. She was known by the code name

'Treasure'. The other was Roger Grosjean, a Frenchman, who went by the code name of 'Fido'.

Nathalie Serguerew was one of the double agents who was part of the Double Cross system and played what has been recognised as a significant part in the deception carried out by MI5 on the Germans to make them unclear as to where the D-Day landings were to take place. She was the niece of Army General Yevgeny Miller. After the Russian Revolution of 1917, her parents decided it was too dangerous to remain, and fled with their family to France. Nathalie was an intelligent girl, who even as a teenager was fluent in French, German and English; she wanted to become a journalist.

She appeared to be drawn to Germany and spent much of the early 1930s travelling there. In 1937 an attempt was made by the *Abwehr* to recruit her as a spy. How the approach came about isn't known, but somebody working for German intelligence clearly saw her potential to make an effective spy. It was a proposition that she was not interested in and so she rejected the approach. But with the outbreak of the Second World War and Germany's speedy advance, first through Poland in 1939 and then France in 1940, Serguerew changed her mind and agreed to work for the *Abwehr* as one of their spies. She was trained by Major Emil Kliemann who taught her the tricks of her trade, so that she would be fully equipped to work and survive as an *Abwehr* agent.

Having been comprehensively trained by Kliemann, she left Germany for Spain in 1943. Although a neutral country during the Second World War, Spain appeared to openly accommodate a number of German spies. Once she arrived in the capital, Madrid, via a friend, she sought out and found an MI5 operative from the British Embassy, informed him that she was a German spy but wanted to work for British Intelligence. As might well be expected in the world of espionage, people were not always believed or taken at face value. Stories had to be checked out, as did dates, locations and names. After the British had completed all of their checks, and her story checked out, she was welcomed with open arms. This was a dangerous scenario for Serguerew, because if MI5 had believed her real loyalty was actually to the Germans, and she was simply trying to infiltrate British Military Intelligence, it is more than likely she would have been killed. Instead she made her way to Britain by sea, stopping off at Gibraltar en route.

Her relationship with her new paymasters quickly became problematical all because of a dog. Before agreeing to work for the *Abwehr*, Sergueiew had a dog named Frisson. She took him with her when she travelled to Madrid and was expecting to keep him with her in her new life in England, but because of strict British quarantine regulations, poor old Frisson was not allowed to accompany her on her journey, instead he remained in Gibraltar while she carried on to England.

Gibraltar had proved problematical in more ways than one. Whilst there, Sergueiew, who had been given the codename 'Treasure' by MI5, met and had an affair with an American airman, Lieutenant Kenneth Larson, although that in itself wasn't the problem. The problem came when, despite only having known the man for a short period, she told him that she worked for British Intelligence. By confiding in Larson, she had run the risk of being a total liability to MI5, to such a degree that she might well have been of no use to them. In that case, she would have been in a potentially difficult situation, because if they had dispensed with her services, what would they have done with a woman known to have previously been a German agent?

The dog obviously meant a lot to her, so much so, that after it failed to arrive in England she threatened her handler, Mary Sherer, that if the dog didn't turn up soon she would stop working for MI5. Sherer compiled a report saying that although she was being troublesome, it was something that she felt could be sorted out. By now it was early May 1944 and D-Day was just a month away; the planning for it could not have been more urgent and everyone involved needed to be focused. But just at that vital time, Sergueiew learnt that Frisson had died in Gibraltar and she was definitely not pleased.

She was acting like a spoiled child who couldn't get her own way, but with D-Day literally just around the corner, the stakes were extremely high. On 17 May 1944 she informed Sherer that she had agreed a secret call sign with Emile Kliemann in Germany, so that she could let him know whether her messages were genuine or whether she was being told what to send. Her naivety was staggering; she obviously did not understand the position she was in, as there was absolutely no way that MI5 would or could, allow her to be compromised with the *Abwehr* back in Germany, nor would they allow her to compromise either the Double-Cross system or the planning for D-Day; there was simply too much at stake. She told Sherer that she blamed MI5 for her dog's death and she wanted revenge for the loss. Despite her annoyance at the death of her beloved animal, she completed her mission by sending messages to her controllers in Germany that the invasion of Nazi occupied Europe would take place across the English Channel at Calais.

A week after D-Day Colonel Robertson informed Sergueiew, in no uncertain terms, that MI5 no longer required her services. He was absolutely fuming. Despite her sacking, and with the war still a year away from its end, MI5 continued to send messages to her handlers in Germany that were purportedly from her.

She returned to France towards the end of 1944 where she enlisted in the French Women's Army Service. She remained angry over what she saw as her treatment by MI5 whom she referred to as gangsters. In 1968 she published her wartime memoirs entitled *Secret Service Rendered*.

Mary Sherer, in the typical stoic British tradition, never spoke of her war time MI5 duties.

Roger Grosjean, who was born in Chalon-sur-Saone on 25 July 1920, had begun the Second World War in the French Air Force, where he remained until November 1942 when he was demobilised, after Germany had successfully invaded the non-occupied area of France. He wanted to make his way to England so that he could join the Free French Air Force, but that was not possible. But not to be deterred, he came up with a plan of convincing the Germans that he was willing to become a spy for them so that they would send him to England. His efforts were successful, and he was sent to England in July 1943.

As was the norm during the Second World War, all foreign nationals entering the Great Britain had to go through what was known as the London Reception Centre at the Royal Patriotic School. This was run by sub section B1D of MI5, and by the end the war, some 30,000 individuals had been checked out at the Centre. On arriving there Grosjean explained his circumstances to his MI5 interrogators and agreed to become a double agent for the British, although his time spent as a spy was relatively short lived, between August 1943 to May 1944. After that he became a flying instructor for the Free French Air Force and was stationed in both Morocco and Algeria teaching those young men who wanted to be pilots how to fly in an American P39 fighter aircraft.

Germany's attempts at espionage, which for them meant carrying out intelligence gathering and acts of sabotage across mainland Britain, only began in earnest after July 1940. There was, however, a belief amongst the British public that German spies were around every corner and hiding under every bed. It was thought they were well trained and had been integrated into British society before the war had even begun. Before 1940 had come to an end, British authorities estimated that no more than twenty-five German agents had arrived in Britain, most of whom weren't even German. The most surprising point as far as the British authorities were concerned, was how poorly trained the German agents appeared to be.

A massive help for MI5 on the espionage front was the breaking of the German Enigma encryption by British mathematicians of the Government Code and Cypher School at Bletchley Park in Buckinghamshire. The first Enigma codes used by the Germans had been broken early in the war, soon after their invasion of Poland, and each time Germany improved the security and codes of their Enigma machines, the diligent and hard-working people at Bletchley Park managed to break them. This meant that with all of Germany's military messages being received and decoded, MI5 had prior knowledge of who the Germans were sending, along with the date, time and location of their arrival in the UK.

As part of the Double-Cross system, once they had deemed a German spy suitable to become a double agent, that individual would be sent to Camp 020, the gloomy, Victorian mansion, that was Latchmere House in Richmond-upon-Thames in south west London. During the First World War the Ministry of Defence had taken it over and turned it into a hospital for officers who were suffering with shell shock. During the Second World

War, it played a totally different role which could not have been further removed from its previous existence. It came under the control of Her Majesty's Prison Service. The only possible indication of the importance of what was going on within its walls, were the uninviting bundles of barbed wire that surrounded it.

The Camp, as it was sometimes referred to, came under the command of Lieutenant Colonel Robin 'Tin Eye' Stephens who, besides being known as not the mildest tempered of individuals, was a natural born interrogator. Unlike some of his peers, he did not shout and scream, nor threaten or pummel, he just sat back in his chair and chatted with the individual opposite him; he was calmness personified. His job was to find out everything he could, every minute little detail about the person who he was going to decide was or wasn't suitable to be used as a double agent.

Some of his traits made him somewhat of an enigma. He was known for the severity of his temper, but he did not care for violent methods being meted out to any of his prisoners. He did not have much time for those who were not British, yet he was half German himself. His nickname, 'Tin Eye', was derived from the monocle he wore, which added to his air of authority.

Camp 020 was run in line with Stephens' morals and personality. In his line of work there was no room for sentiment or having a reputation for being a soft touch, they simply didn't sit well with the end goal of what they were trying to achieve. He did not believe in torture. Those who worked as his interrogators of German agents were told:

> Violence is taboo, for not only does it produce answers to please, but it lowers the standard of information. Never strike a man. In the first place it is an act of cowardice. In the second place, it is not intelligent. A prisoner will lie to avoid further punishment and everything he says thereafter will be based on a false premise.

This is not to suggest that some of Stephens' interrogators did not employ violence or aggression to get a prisoner to talk, just that he did not condone or encourage that type of interrogation. Stephens did, however, use methods which could be interpreted as causing suffering, not in a physical sense but in a psychological one. Latchmere House was eerily silent, intentionally so, which produced a feeling of isolation amongst those detained there. Guards wore tennis shoes, the lack of footsteps covering their very presence, which helped create a feeling of foreboding in the minds of the prisoners. Conversation outside of interrogations was kept to an absolute minimum. Guards did not talk to prisoners, nor give them cigarettes. Sleep deprivation was one of Stephens' favoured tactics. In the book by Gordon Thomas, *Secret Wars: One Hundred Years of British Intelligence Inside MI5 and MI6*, he wrote that Stephens said:

> We are here to crush a spy psychologically. Crush his mind into small pieces, examine those pieces and then if they reveal qualities useful to the war effort, like becoming double agents, they must be rebuilt mentally. Those who do not have the qualities we require will end up on the gallows or before a firing squad in the Tower of London.

Whether the German agents who were interrogated by Stephens fully appreciated or understood the precarious position that they were in once they arrived at Camp 020 is not known. But although they might not have understood, they had to convince Stephens that they were actually going to be double agents, but with their real allegiance to MI5. If Stephens didn't believe that was going to be the case, they wouldn't be brought into the system, the consequence of which had potential dire repercussions. This was war time, not everything was done by the book. There were no hard and fast rules that security agencies played by and espionage was a dangerous business, where capture usually had fatal consequences.

During the war Latchmere House was home, albeit for a relatively short period of time, to some 500 prisoners, many of whom had been German spies. These included James Larratt Battersby, Hugo Bleicher, Costa Caroli, Eddie Chapman, Josef Jakobs, Werner von Janowski, Christiaan Lindemans, Karel Richard Richter, Wulf Schmidt, Duncan Scott-Ford, and Gastao de Freitas Ferraz.

The infamous Lord Haw Haw, or William Joyce, went to Germany where he willingly broadcast Nazi propaganda over the radio from Hamburg. *Germany Calling* was broadcast to both British and American audiences, a programme which was transmitted between 18 September 1939 and 30 April 1945, when Hamburg was captured by the British Army.

At his trial after the war, his defence team argued that as an American citizen and a naturalised German, he could not be convicted of treason against the British Crown – a valid argument, but the prosecution saw it differently. They argued that since he had lied about his nationality to obtain a British passport, and had previously voted in British elections, this meant that he had an allegiance to the king. The jury and the judge agreed and Joyce, having been found guilty of treason, was hanged at Wandsworth prison on 3 January 1946.

There were 120 of those who passed through Latchmere House who were deemed to be suitable enough to be double agents. After the war Stephens' skills were utilised in Germany at an interrogation centre in Bad Nenndorf in Lower Saxony, where he was in charge of some of the most notorious Nazi war criminals. A number of these men were found to have physical injuries whilst others suffered from malnourishment; two of them died after being transferred to a nearby civilian hospital. A number of officers who worked at the interrogation centre, including Stephens, were court martialled on a number of charges. Stephens faced two charges, one of 'professional negligence' and one of 'disgraceful conduct' but was acquitted by a London court.

Those German agents who were deemed suitable to be used as double agents were passed on to Scotsman, Lieutenant Colonel Thomas Argyll Robertson, often referred to by his initials, 'Tar', who led Section B1A. Before the war Robertson had been the case officer of German agent Arthur Owens, otherwise known by the code name of 'Snow'. There is a detailed account of him elsewhere in the book.

Robertson was one of those who understood the benefits of using German spies as double agents. It would certainly provide MI5 with a blueprint of exactly how the *Abwehr* worked, and knowing what information they were after provided an insight into some of the enemy's future military intentions. This knowledge provided MI5 with the ability to totally mislead the Nazis, such as with the invasion of Sicily and the D-Day landings. These two events highlighted just how important a part the Double-Cross system played in winning the war.

As with most things that are new, they are not always quite the finished article, and do not always work out as they were intended to or as it was hoped they would. It was no different for Robertson. Whoever it was in MI5 who chose each of the agents' codenames, obviously had a sense of humour. That was apparent with a couple of his early double agents. There was a George Graf, who had the codename of, 'Giraffe', but for some reason his use in the Double-Cross system was minimal. Then there was the unusually named German agent, Kurt Goose, whose codename was 'Gander' – what else could it possibly have been? He had been sent to England by the Germans with a radio that could only transmit. If it wasn't so serious it would be laughable. Like George Graf, Kurt Goose didn't get used much as a double agent.

With 'Giraffe' and 'Goose' out of the way, things could only get better, or so you would think. Robertson's beginning as a handler of double agents hadn't got off to the most auspicious of beginnings, so he needed a success story and he needed it fast. Step forward Costa Caroli and Wolf Schmidt, the latter of whom was a Danish national. The pair, who were friends and who had undergone their basic spy training together, were also committed Nazis, so not quite the ideal candidates to be looking at to turn into double agents.

Caroli was coerced into becoming a double agent by being told by Robertson that if he didn't acquiesce to MI5's demands, they would shoot Schmidt. Whilst Schmidt was told that Caroli had 'sold him out', which made him so angry that he readily agreed to become a double agent.

It was almost immediately clear to MI5 that using Caroli as a double agent was going to be more trouble than it was worth, if not dangerous as well. He attacked his immediate handler, trying to strangle him, and then made good his escape. This is where it became farcical as he tried to make his get-away on a motorcycle, whilst carrying a canoe. His plan was to get to the coast and then row all the way across the English Channel to Holland. He didn't even get out of London and was arrested when he fell off the motorcycle, in front of a policeman. Not surprisingly once MI5 got him back, they very quickly decided that trying to use him as a double agent was not going to work. Thankfully Schmidt, who had the code name 'Tate', was a totally different individual. He continued to work for Ml5 as an effective double agent right up until the end of the war.

For Robertson, his early attempts of trying to run double agents, had been an 'interesting' experience. Although he learnt a lot from them, he now fully appreciated that he had not chosen an easy profession.

In the early part of the war the main way agents communicated with their handlers, was in writing. But it quickly became obvious that this was not a good means of communication as it could readily be intercepted by postal workers. In addition, many of the addresses the letters were being sent to had already been compromised, making it easier to have the letters intercepted and read. Later in the war the *Abwehr* started supplying their agents with wireless sets, which made matters even easier for MI5. Having all of these captured wirelesses in the same location gave them greater control over what information they sent out. If a difficult or important decision needed to be made, the people who needed to make those decisions were immediately at hand.

Abwehr ciphers had been broken early on in the war, which provided MI5 with a massive advantage over their German counterparts. The ability to be able to read these ciphers not only allowed the British to pick up the content of all the *Abwehr* transmissions, but also allowed them to monitor what information they were sending. If the *Abwehr* had doubts about the loyalty of any of the double agents, then MI5 had early warning of it and could act accordingly to ensure the integrity of the Double-Cross system was not compromised.

One of the delicate aspects of the system was the information that was funnelled by the double agents to their handlers at *Abwehr* headquarters in Hamburg. It could not all just be false information because if it was, the Germans would quickly pick up on it and work out that their agents had been turned by the British and compromised. If this happened, it would mean the end of the Double-Cross system and an important tool in the British and Allied war effort would have been lost. It required in depth consideration to ensure that the information that was passed on, was not going to result in the deaths of British or Allied lives. This was an aspect of the system that made some of those who were responsible for releasing intelligence very nervous indeed.

One of the agents in the Double-Cross system provided his handler, with the say-so of MI5, genuine information about Operation Torch, the Allied invasion of North Africa on 8 November 1942. But because of a built-in delay by the British, it was not supplied until Allied troops had made it ashore, ensuring that no Allied soldiers were wounded or lost their lives. Despite not receiving the information in time for it to be useful to them, the Germans were impressed with the agent concerned.

The Double-Cross system also included operatives who were located in neutral countries such as Spain and Portugal. One agent, **Juan Pujol Garcia**, who had the code name 'Garbo', had managed to convince his handlers in German military intelligence that he was in fact operating out of England and had a number of agents working under him. *Abwehr* ended up putting so much faith in Garcia that they did not send any more agents to England after November 1942. This meant that they were totally dependent on him. He also convinced MI5 that he would be an extremely worthwhile agent for them to use.

The Double-Cross agents were put to good use in the build-up to Operation Fortitude, which was the Allied plan to deceive the Germans into believing that the invasion of Europe would take place elsewhere other than the beaches of Normandy. Part of the deception included agents providing uniform insignia as well as vehicle markings from different areas along the south coast. The deception worked as all of the separate pieces of information received by the *Abwehr* from their agents in England, led them to deduce that the main Allied attack on German occupied Europe, was going to take place across the Straits of Dover and direct to the Pas de Calais region of France. They had received reports that there was a massive Allied Army with all its equipment – the First United States Army Group, under the command of General George S. Patton – that was grouped along the south-east coast of Kent. This did not actually exist; it was all part of the subterfuge the Allies used as part of Operation Quicksilver, to convince the Germans where attacking forces would be leaving from along the English coast.

The deception fooled the Germans so comprehensively, that they kept a staggering fifteen divisions of men and equipment in reserve in the Calais area, even after news had been received from Normandy that there had been an Allied landing there. They had been so impressed with the information received from Juan Pujol Garcia that they awarded him the Iron Cross.

Some of the information which the *Abwehr* received from 'their' agents in relation to troop movements along the south coast of England was factual, but most of it wasn't. Operation Fortitude had three elements to it. There was the breaking of the German Enigma codes, which had happened early on in the war, providing the British with the finite details of a lot of Germany's intentions. Radio signals had been transmitted by the British in such a way that the Germans were certain to overhear and intercept them, giving them the false belief that they knew what the British were up to, when in fact what they were overhearing was false information. The Double-Cross scheme also played a big part in the deception, as the agents involved ultimately succeeded in making the Nazis believe that the invasion of German-occupied Europe was going to take place at the Pas de Calais.

The double agents were again called upon to help the war effort and to save civilian lives when the Nazis began targeting the south east of England with their V1 and V2 flying bombs during the second half of 1944 and the early months of 1945. Double agents Eddie Chapman, code name 'Zig Zag', and Wulf Schmidt, code name 'Tate', were tasked by Duncan Sandys, a minister in Winston Churchill's wartime government and chairman of a War Cabinet Committee for the defence against German flying bombs and rockets. Both agents contacted their handlers in Germany and informed them about how successful the attacks had been. They were told to exaggerate the number of V1s that had fallen in the north and west parts of London, whilst under reporting those that had come down in the south and east of the capital.

In late June 1944 the same two agents informed their handlers in Germany that out of seven V1s aimed at the City of London, only one had fallen south of the River Thames, when in reality, five had fallen in that area. Initially this discrepancy caused a problem, because unbeknown to either of the two agents or the MI5 operatives, the Germans had planted radio transmitters in the weapons, which showed exactly where they had landed. The two agents stuck to their story and thankfully the Germans chose to believe them rather than what their equipment was telling them about where they had landed.

In July 1944 the Germans were informed that there had been considerable damage caused in Southampton, which was not correct, and was something of a surprise for the enemy as the V1s had all been aimed at London.

Special scientific advisor to Winston Churchill, Frederick Lindemann, recommended that the agents inform Germany that there had been heavy losses at Southampton, to put them off attacking London with the possibility of heavy losses being sustained in the capital. When the Cabinet heard of this they ordered the MI5 deception to be stopped, but it continued. The annoyance was with the decision by MI5 that by continuing with the deception, they were in essence saying that the lives of those who lived in Southampton were somehow less important than those who lived in London.

The deception was continued when the more powerful and much faster V2 rockets began falling on London. Because of the continued misinformation being sent back to Germany, the V2s were gradually directed away from central London and off to the east. Once again this met with some resistance, as people died no matter where these bombs dropped. For many it left a nasty taste because the work of the MI5 agents hadn't prevented the bombings, but simply changed the location of the victims.

The following is a list of known Double-Cross agents who were used by British military intelligence during the course of the Second World War.

Artist – His real name was **Johnny Jebsen**, who was kidnapped whilst in Lisbon by the Germans shortly before the Normandy landings, and is believed to have been taken back to Berlin where he was tortured. He spent time in a concentration camp before he disappeared towards the end of the war. It is believed that he was murdered by the Nazis.

Balloon – A man by the name of **Dick Metcalfe** who was part of the Double-Cross system between May 1941 and November 1943. That is all there is known of his life as an agent.

Basket – **Joseph Lenihan** was born in Ireland but left there sometime in the early 1930s to live in America, where he stayed for a couple of years before returning to Ireland. Around the time of the outbreak of the Second World War he turned up on the island of Jersey working as a farm labourer and it was whilst trying to escape from the German-occupied island, on a stolen boat, that he was arrested. It was whilst he was in the custody of the Gestapo that he was approached to become a German agent. He was parachuted into Ireland in July 1941 and promptly handed himself in to the British authorities in Northern Ireland. He was eventually interrogated by officers from MI5, and although deemed unsuitable for use in the Double-Cross system, was allocated the code name 'Basket'.

Beetle – **Petur Thomsen**, who was based in Iceland, although there appears to be no other information about him.

Biscuit – His real name was **Sam McCarthy**.

Bootle – Jointly handled by Britain's Secret Intelligence Services and France's Deuxième Bureau.

Bronx – **Elvira Chaudoir** was the daughter of a South American diplomat and was part of the Double-Cross system between October 1942 and May 1945.

Brutus – was a Polish Army officer, **Roman Czerniawski**, who was part of the Double-Cross system between October 1942 and January 1945. He agreed to work for the *Abwehr* after the Franco–Polish underground espionage network that he had been working for had been exposed by a Gestapo informant.

Careless – **Clark Korab** was a Polish pilot, who had been captured by the Germans in the early months of the war. He was very ill-disciplined which greatly curtailed his usefulness as a double agent.

Carrot – Although his name is not recorded, he was believed to be a Polish airman, who was only part of the Double-Cross system for seven months between June and December 1942.

Celery – **Walter Dicketts** was sent by MI5 into Nazi Germany in early 1941 to infiltrate the *Abwehr* and find out any information about an impending invasion of Britain. His job was to convince the Germans he was a traitor willing to sell out his country in return for cash, whilst actually working for MI5. His is a colourful story in its own right. He was quite a character, having joined the Royal Naval Air Service during the First World War, he became a pilot in 1917. He went on to serve numerous prison sentences, mainly for fraud, and is believed to have been betrayed to the Germans by Arthur Owens, during the early years of the Second World War. Dicketts survived his time in German hands and made it back home to England.

Charlie – Only known by his surname, **Kiener**, who was a German born in Britain.

Cheese – **Renato Levi**, worked for the *Abwehr*, Britain's MI5, and the Italian Military Secret Service, *Servizio Informazioni Militare*. He also had a reputation as a womaniser and being a bit of a playboy, in keeping with his good looks. An Italian Jew, he was born in Genoa in 1902 and during the Second World War gained himself another reputation, that of being an outstanding spy who did much for the Allied war effort. Soon after the outbreak of the Second World War he was recruited by the *Abwehr*, who remarkably had not discovered his Jewish connections. He immediately informed the British authorities of the German approach and became part of the Double-Cross system. He was undoubtedly one of Britain's most effective wartime spies.

Cobweb – **Ib Arnason Riis**, was born on 15 January 1915 and during the Second World War was based in Iceland. When Germany invaded Denmark, Riis, who had been a ship's captain before the war, found himself stuck. He was approached by the *Abwehr* and asked to take a ship to Iceland, a request to which he reluctantly agreed as he wanted to get home to his beloved country. When he found that he had been lied to, he refused to go, but eventually he was dropped off by German submarine *U-252* at Langanes in Iceland, and immediately buried his *Abwehr*-issued gun and wireless. His cover story was that he was a German Merchant Naval officer. He eventually found his way to a British Army outpost and gave himself up, before being taken to Reykjavik to be interrogated. He was taken to Langanes to recover his wireless and gun, partly to help prove his story, and also because if he was going to work for the British as a double agent, he would need his radio.

So impressed were the *Abwehr* with the information Riis supplied, that they awarded him the Iron Cross, both 1st and 2nd Class. He worked for MI5 and was tasked with radio information on convoy PQ17 to the Germans. The plan was to use the convoy, which had left Iceland on 27 June 1942, to attract Germany's battleship, *Tirpitz*, and then for the British Royal Navy to attack her. It also helped provide Riis with credibility with his *Abwehr* handlers in Germany.

Dreadnought – Ivan Popov was the elder brother of the more famous Dusan Popov, whose codename in the Double-Cross system was **Tricycle**. Ivan Popov was born in Titel, in what was then Austria-Hungary. The family were extremely wealthy, their money coming from banking, factories, mines and retail businesses.

Dragonfly – Hans George was an Englishman, born to German parents. As part of the Double-Cross system, he provided the Germans with weather reports, troop movements and anything to do with Allied military matters. He worked as a double agent between March 1941 and January 1944.

Father – a Belgian pilot by the name of **Henri Arents**. He had been tasked by the Germans with stealing a British aircraft and flying it back to Germany. He served as a double agent for two years between June 1941 and 1943.

Fido – I have written in some detail about **Roger Grosjean**, elsewhere in this book.

Freak – Marquis Franco de Bona was Yugoslavian, who was part of Dusan Popov's network and a member of the Double-Cross system between December 1943 and May 1944.

Gander – Hans Reysen landed in the UK on 3 October 1940 and was only used as part of the Double-Cross system for a few weeks.

His mission was to report on defences in the north-west of England and the state of civilian morale.

Garbo – Juan Pujol Garcia was Spanish and a very interesting character, who at the end of the war was awarded the MBE by Britain, presented to him 25 November 1944 by King George VI, and the Iron Cross 2nd Class, by the Germans, on 29 July 1944. Those two awards alone show just how good an agent he was. In 1931 Pujol did his six months of compulsory service in the Spanish military in a cavalry unit, the 7th Regiment of Light Artillery. He knew he was unsuited for a military career, hating horse-riding and claiming to lack the 'essential qualities of loyalty, generosity and honour'. This gave him some idea of what life for a soldier was like.

He started out as an independent spy and at the beginning of the war, Pujol decided that he had to do something good and positive for the sake of mankind. He wasn't driven by money, greed, idealistic political doctrine, or personal fame and glory. As a Spaniard he opposed Franco and his regime and the damage and harm that he saw it was doing to his country and its people. He approached the British authorities on three separate occasions to work for them as a spy, but they showed no interest. Rather than being put off by this rejection, he came up with a novel way of making them listen to him and to take his attempts to work for them seriously. He decided to establish himself as a German spy and then contact the British again so that he could work for them as a double agent.

His method of achieving this was truly remarkable. He simply created a character who purportedly worked for the Spanish government, who also just happened to be fanatically pro-Nazi. He managed to acquire a fake Spanish diplomatic passport by pretending to work for the Spanish embassy in Lisbon, Portugal. Armed with all of this he then approached an *Abwehr* agent in Lisbon called Friedrich Knappe-Ratey telling him that he wanted to work for the German authorities. His story was believed and after being provided with a crash course in how to be a spy, he was given £600, told to move to Britain and set up a network of agents. Instead, he moved to Lisbon and fed back information that he had read about in newspapers and had seen on wartime newsreels. He backed up these reports by adding that he was travelling around Britain.

His mission was to report on all and any military developments that he saw. He used writing, wireless messages and couriers as means of delivering messages to his *Abwehr* handlers in Germany, during his three years of being part of the Double-Cross system.

Besides the made-up spying, he also created a number of fictitious sub-agents who supposedly lived in different parts of the country. Because some of the messages he sent to the *Abwehr* were transmitted by way of wireless messages, they were picked up by Britain's Ultra programme. This was the name given by British Military Intelligence to wartime signals intelligence that had been obtained by breaking high-level encrypted radio and teleprinter communications at the British Government's Code and Cypher School at Bletchley Park. Because Pujol's reports seemed so realistic it caused something of a panic at MI5, so much so that they set up a full-scale investigation in the belief that there was a German spy running amok across the country, although they couldn't work out how that was possible.

In February 1942, just after the debacle at Pearl Harbor had seen America enter the Second World War, Pujol contacted the United States Naval attaché's office in Lisbon, where he spoke with Lieutenant Patrick Demorest, offering his services to the Americans. Demorest immediately saw something in him and contacted his counterparts within British intelligence.

His real value became apparent to the British when they saw the number of ships the German navy allocated to finding a convoy that did not exist, that had been reported to them by Pujol. MI5 made contact with Pujol in Lisbon and discovered that he would be only too happy to work for them as a double agent. On 24 April 1942, he arrived in England, and was initially given the code name of, 'Bovril'. He was then allocated an MI5 officer, Tomas Harris, to work alongside him. Harris and his colleagues in British Military Intelligence quickly realised what a find they had in Pujol. Because of this they decided to change his codename from 'Bovril' to 'Garbo' in keeping with his ability to act his way out of any given situation, just like the actress he had been named after, Greta Garbo.

In total, Pujol and Harris sent more than 300 letters to the *Abwehr* via a post office box number in Lisbon, from Pujol and his pretend network of spies. Collectively, the information Pujol supplied so impressed the Germans that they did not look to recruit any more agents to send to England, which in itself was a truly remarkable achievement.

Garbo was unique in that he wanted to become a spy to help to bring about an end to the war. The British had turned him down on more than one occasion; he became a double agent just to prove his worth and not because he was first and foremost a German agent forced into becoming a double agent after having been captured and turned.

The information that Garbo supplied to the Germans was a combination of lies, truth that had little or no real military value, or information that was real, valuable military intelligence which by the time the Germans received it, had already taken place. An example of this would be sending intelligence via the post so that the date of the posting would show that it was sent in plenty of time prior to an incident taking place, but which had been purposely delayed by British military intelligence.

An example of just good Pujol was at being a spy is shown when he was questioned by the Germans about a major fleet movement of the Royal Navy that hadn't been reported by Pujol or any of his network of spies. Pujol replied that his fictitious agent in Liverpool, the one who should have reported the fleet movement, had been taken ill just prior to the event and had therefore been unable to report on it. To give his claim some credence, Pujol reported to his German spy masters, a few weeks later that the agent had subsequently died. To make that claim even more believable, Pujol arranged for an obituary to appear about the man and how he had died, in a Liverpool newspaper. With an added twist of humour, Pujol even convinced the *Abwehr* to pay the man's equally non-existent widow, a pension.

Pujol was informed by the *Abwehr* in January 1944 that they had received information that the Allies were planning a large-scale invasion of German occupied Europe, but that they didn't know where or when it would take place. They tasked Pujol with passing on to them any information that he might discover that might be connected to the invasion. They were, of course, talking about Operation Overlord and the D-Day landings in Normandy. This gave the Allies the opportunity to deceive the Germans into thinking the invasion would take place across the Straits of Dover, but they also wanted to preserve Garbo's credibility with the enemy.

In the early hours of 6 June 1944, Garbo transmitted a message that he was waiting on one his agents who had some very important information for him, but by the time the German wireless operators replied it was 8am. This then allowed Garbo to provide some quite detailed information about the invasion, which by then didn't matter as it had already begun. As it was a mistake by the Germans, not responding until 8am, their belief was that Garbo's message would have been exactly the same if received in the early hours of 6 June, and therefore would have given advanced detailed information of the actual invasion of Europe.

Three days after D-Day, Garbo sent another detailed message which spoke of the number of divisions that were forming up in England, making specific reference to the American General Patton and the phoney First United States Army Group, made up of some eleven divisions, supposedly situated in the south-east of England. They had not taken part in the Normandy landings, and therefore Normandy should be considered as no more than a diversion for the main attack that would take place across the Straits of Dover. In the belief that this information was correct, the Germans held two armoured and nineteen infantry divisions in the Pas de Calais area, so convinced were they that that was where the main Allied invasion force would come ashore. Two months after D-Day, they still had massive numbers of troops and large quantities of equipment in the Pas de Calais area. This deception was all part of what was known as Operation Fortitude.

Pujol had made up a total of twenty-seven totally fictitious agents, giving them all names, characters, personalities, individual traits and reasons for doing what they were doing. In total Pujol received nearly US $350,000 for his network of non-existent spies.

Gelatine – an Austria woman by the name of **Gerda Sullivan**, who was sent to Britain to gather political information and was part of the Double-Cross scheme between May 1941 and May 1945.

Gilbert – **André Latham**, who was jointly handled by the British Secret Intelligence Service and the French Deuxième Bureau.

Giraffe – **Georges Graf** was Czechoslovakian. His job was to report on anything to do with the Royal Air Force.

GW – **Gwilym Williams** was Welsh and worked as a double agent between October 1939 and February 1942. His main attribute was that of sabotage.

Hamlet – was an Austrian by the name of **Dr Koestler**.

Hatchet – went by the name of **Albert de Jaeger**.

Jeff – Whose real name was **Olav Klausen**, was a Norwegian, who was part of the Double-Cross system between April 1941 and December 1944, although he was imprisoned from August 1941 onwards.

Josef – **Yuri Smelkov** was a Russian. His mission was to report on shipping and convoy movements. He was part of the Double-Cross system between August 1942 and December 1944.

Le Chatte – or in English 'The She Cat', was **Mathilde Carré**, a French resistance fighter, who became a double agent. After the fall of France she met Roman Czerniawski, a Polish air force captain, who was part of the Franco-Polish Interallié espionage network. On 17 November 1941, after the group had been betrayed by a Gestapo informant, many of their number, including Carré and Czerniawski were arrested. Carré was interrogated by the *Abwehr*'s Hugo Bleicher, threatened with death and then offered a financial reward, before agreeing to become an *Abwehr* agent. She allegedly gave up the names of everybody she knew who were part of the Franco-Polish Interallié network.

After she was released, members of the French Resistance suspected that she might be working for the Germans. At the time she was in a relationship with a member of the resistance unit who worked for the British Special Operations Executive. She confessed and expected the worst, but instead the SOE operative, Pierre de Vomecourt, came up with a plan to turn the situation around on the Germans. She managed to convince the *Abwehr* to send her to London to infiltrate the British SOE. After some discussion, they agreed to her request. Along with de Vomecourt she was sent to London and MI5 took her on for a while as a double agent, but once her usefulness had ran out she was arrested and imprisoned, initially at HM Prison Holloway and then at HM Prison Aylesbury, where she remained for the rest of the war. There she became a prison informant against her fellow inmates.

After the war she was deported to France, where she was put on trial for treason. On 7 January 1949, she was found guilty of treason and sentenced to death, later commuted to 20 years imprisonment. She was finally released in September 1954.

Lambert – was also known as **Nikitov**, a Russian national.

Lipstick – **Josef Terradellas**, a Spaniard, whose mission it was to observe Allied troop movements and numbers in the UK. He was part of the Double-Cross system, between November 1942 and March 1944.

Meteor – **Eugen Sostaric**, a Yugoslav patriot, who the Germans attempted to get to do a Triple Cross. He was active as an agent between April 1943 and May 1944. His mission was to concentrate on naval related matters.

Monoplane – **Paul Jeannin** had previous code names of 'Jaques' and 'Twit', whilst the Germans had given him the code name of 'Normandie'. He was active between April 1943 and May 1944.

Moonbeam – was based in Canada. His name is unknown.

Mullett – was a man by the name of Thornton, who was British but born in Belgium, and worked in Brussels as an insurance agent. He was active between December 1941 and May 1944.

Mutt and Jeff – Otherwise known as **Helge Moe** and **Tor Glad**, were two Norwegians. Moe was also known by the name of **Jack Berg**. Their mission was to provide information of a military nature and to commit acts of sabotage. They arrived in England on 7 April 1941 and were detained and offered the chance to become part of the Double-Cross system, which they were involved in between April 1941 and February 1944.

Peppermint – **Jose Brugada** was a Spanish Embassy official. His mission was to gather information on matters such as civilian morale, military matters, factories and aircraft information. He was active between December 1941 and April 1943, and sent his messages via the diplomatic bag.

Puppet – Mr Fanto, who was British and the manager of a Colgate toothpaste factory. He was active between April 1943 and May 1944.

Rainbow – Gunther Schutz was parachuted into Ireland on 12 March 1941. He wasn't part of the Double-Cross system as he did not come under the auspices of Britain's MI5.

Rover – was an unnamed Polish sailor, who had been captured by the Germans during their invasion of Poland in 1939. His mission was to provide information concerning locations of aircraft factories, and Luftwaffe air raid damage. He was active as a Double-Cross agent between May 1944 and May 1945. At the end of the war he was handed over to the Polish Army.

Scruffy – was a Belgian by the name of **Alphonse Timmerman**.

Shepherd – was a Frenchman, his mission was to report on suppliers, manufacturers, the attitude of miners and railway employees.

The Snark – was **Maritza Mihailovic**, a Yugoslavian domestic servant, who was part of the Double-Cross system between November 1943 and May 1945. Her mission was to report back on food prices and living conditions for the civilian population.

Sniper – not much is known about him other than he was a pilot in the Belgian air force. He was tasked with reporting on aircraft and methods used in anti-submarine warfare. That definitely comes into the category of, 'how was he supposed to find that out?' In December 1944 he was handed over to the 21st Army Group, although it is not clear why. Between June 1944 and August 1945, the 21st Army Group operated in Northern France, Luxembourg, Belgium, the Netherlands and Germany.

Snow – There is a separate chapter on **Arthur Owens**, later in this book.

Spider – was an operative who was based in Iceland, it is not known whether male or female.

Springbok – was **Hans von Kotze**. I can only assume, with the code name being the same as the national emblem of South Africa and the name that Kotze is of the same nationality.

Stephan – Klein was his name but that is all I could find out about him.

Summer – Gosta Caroli appears elsewhere in the book.

Sweet William – was **William Jackson**. He was British but worked out of the Spanish Embassy in London. He was part of the Double-Cross system for a year between August 1941 and August 1942. His mission was to report on civilian morale and the food situation.

Tate – Wulf Schmidt appears later in the book.

Teapot – was part of the Double-Cross system between January 1943 and 1945, but I have no name for him. He was a triple cross agent who provided information for the Admiralty.

Treasure – was **Nathalie Sergueiew**, also known as Lily Sergeyev. She was a French woman of Russian origin. There is more about her elsewhere in the book. She was active in the Double-Cross system between August 1943 and December 1944, with her mission to look out for any invasion news and information of a military nature.

Tricycle – was **Dusan Popov**, who was born in Titel, Austria-Hungary in 1912, into a wealthy family. In 1934 Popov enrolled in the University of Freiburg to study Law. Germany had only been under Nazi rule since 1933 but at the time, Popov had no interest in politics. He had decided on Freiburg University, because it was relatively close to his native country and he also saw it as a good opportunity to improve his German. The early days of Nazi atrocities in Germany had already begun with the organized mass book burnings, and the first of the concentration camps had already been created along with the systematic persecution of the Jews.

In the summer of 1937, Popov successfully completed his doctoral thesis. His way of celebrating was to take a trip to the romantic city of Paris, but before he could leave, he was arrested by the Gestapo. His 'crime' was that the Gestapo believed he was a Communist. He had been followed by some of their undercover agents who questioned those he spoke to. Popov was held in the Freiburg prison without any trial or any evidence being presented. Jebsen, on hearing news of his friend's arrest, called Popov's father and he contacted the Prime Minister of Yugoslavia,

Above left: Winston Churchill.

Above right: Karel Richter.

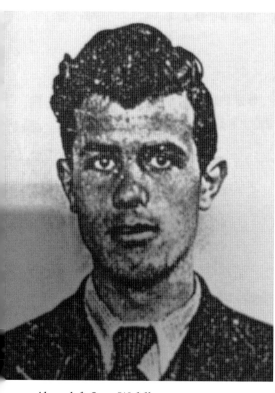

Above left: Jose Waldberg.

Above right: Charles van den Kieboom.

Above left: Sjoerd Pons.

Above right: The Old Bailey.

Lt-Colonel William Edward Hinchley-Cooke.

Wandsworth Prison.

Above left: Hermann Gortz.

Above right: Josef Jakobs.

Heinkel He 111.

Tower of London.

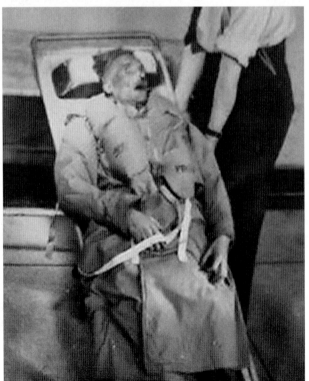

Above left: Lieutenant-Colonel Robin "Tin Eye" Williams.

Above right: John Cecil Masterman.

Left: Glyndwr Michael.

Grave of Glyndwr Michael.

Roger Grosjean.

Emile Kliemann.

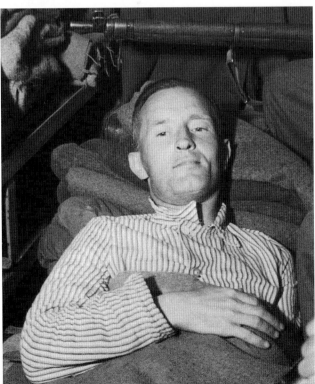

Above: Camp 020 Latchmere
House. (*Creative Commons
Attribution-Share Alike 3.0
Unported license*)

Right: William Joyce.

Invasion of North Africa.

Above left: Juan Pujol Garcia.

Above right: Johnny Jebsen.

Walter Dicketts.

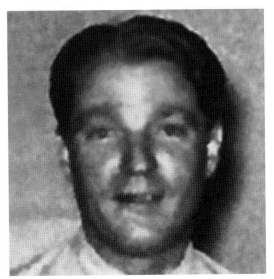

Above left: Renato Levi.

Above right: Dusan Popov.

Admiral Wilhelm Canaris.
(*German National Archives*)

Laszlo Almasay.

Above: Zossen Headquarters.

Right: Engelbertus Fukken.

Arthur Owens.

German Wireless Transmitter.

Above: Mauser 6.35mm Pistol.

Right: Vera Eriksen.

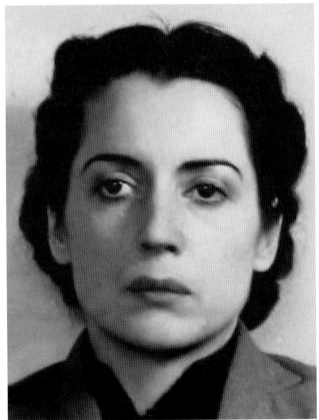

Kenneth Berry and Alfred
Minchin in German uniforms.

Eddie Chapman

Milan Stojadinovic, who raised the issue directly with Hermann Göring. After having spent eight days in prison, Popov was released on the proviso that he left Germany within twenty-four hours. He did not hang about, going straight to his lodgings, collected his belongings and caught a train to Switzerland.

Having arrived in Basel, he found his friend Jebsen waiting for him on the station platform, who was keen to inform him of the role he played in securing his release. Popov expressed his gratitude and told him that if he was ever in need of similar help himself, he only had to ask. It was three years before Jebsen called Popov to ask for his help. He said that he needed some help to obtain a Yugoslav shipping licence in relation to his family's shipping company, but that he first needed to go to Berlin to collect some documentation to help him acquire the licence. Other than waiting for Jebsen to return, Popov wasn't sure what it was he was actually doing to repay his friend.

Two weeks later Jebsen returned to Belgrade and told Popov that he had in fact joined the German *Abwehr* as a researcher. Popov was surprised as he knew his friend had strong anti-Nazi views.

Popov approached a passport control officer, Clement Hope, who worked at the British legation in Yugoslavia, and Hope responded by enrolling him as a double agent and giving him the code name 'Scoot', which as we now know, was later changed to 'Tricycle'. Hope encouraged Popov to stay close to his friend Jebsen and see if he could find out anything useful from him. It was through his connection with Jebsen that he was also accepted by the *Abwehr* to work for them. Clement Hope couldn't have been happier.

Once London had confirmed and authorised Popov as a double agent, he was moved to London. His business activities were an excellent cover and helped cover up the real reason for his foreign travel. Despite the war, there was a regular civilian air service from the UK to Lisbon in Portugal, which allowed him to meet up with his *Abwehr* handler and provide him with MI6 approved information that was relevant to the war, of little strategic purpose but sufficient to keep the Germans happy. When he was then tasked by them to find out specific information, this was of great value to the British as they then had a strong indication of future German plans. He was part of Operation Fortitude, the plan to make the Germans believe that the invasion of Europe was going to take place at the Pas de Calais.

The *Abwehr* sent Popov to the United States in 1941 to set up a spy network; their collective role was to try and gain intelligence on a number of nominated targets of interest. One of these was Pearl Harbor, on the Hawaiian island of Oahu. Popov had been instructed to find out as much as he could about the American defences at Pearl Harbor. Via official channels Popov made contact with the FBI on 12 August 1941, to inform them about the German interest in Pearl Harbor. It was obvious to both parties that a request for such detailed information about the American base could only mean one thing – an imminent attack.

The then head of the FBI, J. Edgar Hoover, either didn't pass the information on to his superiors, or if he did, they decided to do nothing about it. The consequences of their lack of action on the matter have been recorded in history since Sunday, 7 December 1941.

Hoover didn't like Popov because he knew that he was a double agent and he was distrustful and suspicious of him.

Washout – Ernesto Simoes, the son of a man who worked at the British Embassy in Lisbon. He was only active between June and December 1942 and had been tasked by the *Abwehr* to find out what he could about troop movements and aircraft production.

Watchdog – Werner Alfred Waldemar von Janowski was an interesting case, as he was actually arrested in Canada having been dropped off by the German submarine *U-518* at around 5am on 9 November 1942, off the coast of New Carlisle in Quebec, Canada. He was arrested within a matter of hours of coming ashore whilst travelling on a train from New Carlisle to Montreal. He was held in Canada for another nine months before being sent to England in August 1943, where he was held at Camp 020. He remained there until the end of the war. In July 1945 he was repatriated to Germany, where he was put in an internment camp in the British Zone before being finally released in 1947.

Weasel – a Belgian doctor, who was active between May and December 1942. He was not one of MI5's success stories, and it is believed that he tried his best to let the Germans know that he had been 'turned'. He may well have been successful in his attempts, as in December 1942, the Germans stopped replying to any of his reports.

The Worm – a Yugoslavian, known by the name of **Stefan Zeiss**, but it is believed that his real name may well have been Jean. He was active between July 1943 and January 1944 and had been tasked with gathering all military connected information.

Zigzag – There is a separate chapter on Eddie Chapman, later in this book.

Chapter Five

Operation Lena

Operation Sealion was Nazi Germany's plan to invade Britain during the latter months of 1940. Six divisions of German Army Group A were tasked with landing in the Bexhill, Folkstone and Ramsgate areas of Kent, whilst a further four divisions of the group were due to land at Brighton in Sussex and the Isle of Wight in Hampshire. Further along the coast, three divisions of Army Group B were to land at Lyme Bay in Dorset.

The Kent section of Army Group A would then advance towards south-east London, as far up as Maldon in Essex and St Albans in Hertfordshire. The other part of Army Group A would make their way towards west London and meet up with their colleagues who had landed in Kent, so that together they could encircle London. Army Group B was tasked with taking control of Bristol.

The plan was tactically sound and certainly achievable, but for it to be able to take place, Germany needed to have control of the skies over the English Channel, so that her invading troops would not be wiped out by the aircraft of the Royal Air Force. There was another element to the operation which had nothing to do with military defeats or victories, but high tides. Between August and November 1940, there were really only four sets of high tide dates when the Germans could sensibly look to carry out their intended invasion. These were: 5 to 9 August, 2 to 7 September, 1 to 6 October and 30 October to 4 November 1940. The first of those two high tides was just eight weeks after the evacuations at Dunkirk, leaving Britain with a shortage of battle-ready fighting men and equipment from rifles and ammunition to artillery pieces, trucks and lorries.

Although Churchill said that he did not feel the invasion threat was a creditable one, he instructed the preparation of extensive defences along the beaches of the south coast of England, to try and neutralise the threat.

On 14 May 1940 the civilian-manned Local Defence Volunteers, later better known as the Home Guard, were created to assist with defending Britain.

Operation Lena was meant to help pave the way for the eventual invasion. It came under the control of Germany's military intelligence agency, the *Abwehr*, which as part of Operation Lena, sent twelve spies to England in September 1940. In a night-time operation, some were parachuted in whilst others rowed ashore in rubber boats after having been dropped off by a German submarine. The entire operation was somewhat confusing and ended up being as incompetent as it was possible to be.

The confusion comes in the shape of the timeline of events. In early August, and despite the dates of the expected high tides in the English Channel, the German High Command agreed that the invasion of Britain would begin on 15 September 1940, but because of potential issues this would cause for the German Imperial Navy, the date was put back until 20 September. This was despite Adolf Hitler telling his generals on 14 August 1940 that he would not attempt to go ahead with the invasion of Britain if he believed it was too dangerous. At a conference in Germany on 14 September, Hitler announced to his military commanders that he intended to reconsider the decision to go ahead with the invasion of Britain on the agreed date; this was because the Royal Air Force had still not been defeated and, without air superiority, the invasion simply could not go ahead. Just three days later on 17 September, a meeting took place between Hitler, Field Marshal Karl Rudolf Gerd von Rundstedt and Reich Marshal Hermann Göring. After Hitler had listened intently to his subordinates' views and opinions, and with the knowledge that the Luftwaffe had still not gained control of the skies over the English Channel, he gave the order for the postponement of Operation Sealion, and ordered the immediate dispersal of all ships which were on standby for the invasion to ensure they were not damaged or lost in air attacks.

On 12 October 1940 a directive by Hitler was issued releasing all forces that had been earmarked for Operation Sealion, making them free and available to be utilised in other theatres of war.

Keeping those dates in mind, let us now look at Operation Lena, the *Abwehr*'s plan to land twelve agents in Britain during early September 1940 – their mission, to gather intelligence on British defences along the south coast of England, to pave the way for, and to help determine if, the invasion of Britain, that would have been one of Germany's most important operations of the Second World War, was viable. What purpose they could have sensibly served, I could not even begin to guess at. Remember, this wasn't a group of highly trained, multi-skilled, battle-hardened German special forces operatives that had been dropped in ahead of an invading force. It was a group of civilian, and it could be argued, amateurish, 'spies' who were being sent on their very first mission, ahead of an invading Army. That just doesn't make any sense at all. Was this an attempt by rogue elements within the *Abwehr* to undermine Operation Sealion, or to send a message to the British about what was about to take place?

So, with Hitler having doubts about the viability of Operation Sealion as early as 14 August 1940, why were the *Abwehr* sending a group of twelve agents to Britain in connection with that very operation less than a month later. Was Operation Sealion actually ever a reality or was it just one big bluff at attempting to get Britain to negotiate a peace agreement, so that Germany could focus on occupying the rest of Europe, beginning with Russia.

The commander of the Luftwaffe, General Adolf Josef Ferdinand Galland, who flew 705 combat missions during the Second World War, claimed that invasion plans of Britain were never serious, and when it was officially called off the Wehrmacht were greatly relieved. Gerd von Rundstedt was of the exact same opinion. He claimed that Hitler never seriously intended to go ahead with an invasion of Britain, but rather was hoping with the fall of France and the subsequent evacuations at Dunkirk, Britain would be more than happy to make peace, possibly believing that she wouldn't be so lucky a third time.

As early as November 1939, staff of the German Imperial Navy produced a report on the possible future invasion of Britain. It highlighted two obvious aspects which if Germany had not acquired, would not allow the operation to go ahead safely – air and naval superiority, which Germany did not have nor was likely to obtain. Grand Admiral Raeder did not think Germany would be a position to carry out such an invasion until around April 1941. Like Hitler he believed that there were other ways Germany could make Britain seek peace terms rather than having to invade. Raeder's thinking was as far removed from invading Britain as one could consider. He spoke of German forces attacking and overrunning Malta and the Suez Canal, which would then allow them a gateway to be able to link up with Japanese forces, which would bring about the total defeat of British interests in the Far East, something which the Japanese managed of their own accord in February 1942. If the two nations joined forces, he felt that this would also prevent American forces from being able to use British bases, in the event of them entering the war.

All that is known for certain is that Operation Sealion never took place. Over the years since the Second World War, there has been much debate about whether such an invasion would have ever worked. It certainly wouldn't have done if the Germans did not have control of the air and sea. As was seen by the subsequent D-Day landings on the Normandy beaches in France, it required a herculean effort logistically to ensure the invasion was a success; not just with men, but with ammunition, equipment, vehicles, replacement troops, food and water. To help facilitate these requirements the Allies dragged Mulberry Harbours across the English Channel, which were then set down close to the Normandy beaches, to be able to support and supply the infantrymen doing the fighting. Was Germany that prepared in 1940? I do not believe they were. Without such facilities they would have needed to use existing harbours along the south coast of England. This leads to the obvious question, were any of these locations actually big enough to be able to deal with the massive amounts of supplies Germany would have needed to be able to sustain her invasion of Britain?

Returning to the issues surrounding Operation Lena and the twelve German spies who arrived in England in early September 1940, they really were terrible spies and poorly trained ones at that. The standard of their skills and abilities was so bad, it is hard to understand how *Abwehr* chiefs considered them of a good enough quality to send them on such an important mission.

The head of the *Abwehr* in Hamburg at the time was Herbert Wichmann. His boss, and in fact the overall chief of the organization, was Admiral Wilhelm Franz Canaris, who had been in charge since 1935. In the early days of the Nazi party, Canaris had high hopes for Germany under Hitler, but by the outbreak of hostilities he had seen the error of his ways and spent the rest of the war trying his best to undermine Hitler and the Nazis.

In February 1944, Hitler, on the insistence of Heinrich Himmler, sacked Canaris and disbanded the entire *Abwehr* organization. Soon afterwards Canaris was placed under house arrest, but released in June 1944 and given a job in Berlin as the head of the impressively named Special Staff for Mercantile Warfare and Economic Combat Measures. But this period of freedom and re-endorsement by the Nazi party was short lived and he was arrested on 23 July 1944.

On 20 July 1944, just three days before Canaris's arrest, an attempt was made to assassinate Adolf Hitler at the Wolf's Lair headquarters near Rastenburg in East Prussia. The plot was the combined efforts of different elements within the German resistance, and an attempt by them to gain political control of Germany and to try and broker a peace deal with the Allies.

The bomb that Claus von Stauffenberg left in a briefcase during a meeting between Hitler and a number of his senior officers, exploded, but Hitler survived. The incident has become known as the 20 July plot. The Gestapo, or the secret police of the Nazi Party, left no stone unturned in their efforts to discover all those who were involved in the plot. By the time they had finished their enquiries, they had arrested more than 7,000 people. Of these 4,980 were executed for their involvement in the plot.

Colonel Georg Hansen, who replaced Canaris as the head of Germany's Military Intelligence, was one of those involved in the German resistance and was arrested in the immediate aftermath of the 20 July plot. On the day of the assassination attempt against Hitler, Hansen had been in Michelau, at the baptism of one of his daughters, a reasonable excuse for not being at the meeting with Hitler in the Wolf's Lair, but it didn't save him. He returned to Berlin on 21 July and was arrested the next day by Heinrich Müller, the head of the Gestapo. During his intensive interrogation, Hansen broke down and confessed his part in the plot against Hitler and, in doing so, also implicated Canaris.

Herbert Wichmann was in a prime position, as the man in charge of the *Abwehr*'s Hamburg 'office' to reduce the effectiveness of any and all German agents sent to Britain. It would appear that this was definitely the case with Operation Lena. If the *Abwehr* had been infiltrated and run by members of the German resistance, who were determined to wrestle their nation back from the evil grip of Nazism, this would explain the appalling standard of the agents it was sending to Britain. One can only conclude this to be the case, as it is the only sensible explanation as to the abstract failure of these agents to make any kind of impact on their missions having once arrived in Britain. But if, as I believe, the *Abwehr* were intentionally sending inadequately trained or totally inept agents to Britain, it would go a long way to proving that not only were Wichmann and Canaris attempting to bring down the Nazis from within by their actions, but many members of the *Abwehr* must have been working alongside them. It would not have been possible for somebody within the organization not to have known what was going on and to notice that poorly trained and ill-prepared agents were being sent to Britain with little or no possibility of succeeding in their missions.

Certainly none of those agents who were sent as part of Operation Lena would have been of any help to a large invading German amphibious force, because they had all been arrested. This is the theory that is put forward by German historian Monika Siendentopf, who in 2014 wrote a book entitled *Operation Sealion: Resistance inside German Intelligence.*

In relation to Canaris and Wichmann's actions about trying to undermine Hitler's 'intended' invasion of Britain as part of Operation Sealion, the question is why? Was it because they wanted to make peace with Britain, or because they felt that to go ahead with the operation was not only futile, but would lead to the unnecessary deaths of thousands of young German fighting men.

Wichmann was totally against Hitler's 'plan' to invade Britain, although he would understandably never voice that opinion in public. He believed that any such attempt would not only fail, but could have potentially devastating effects, not only on German morale, but the country's ability to achieve her other intentions in the war. Both Wichmann and Canaris knew that not only was it futile to voice criticism of Hitler's plans, but it was also personally very dangerous. A minimum response from Hitler in such circumstances would usually result in an individual being sacked from his position.

The case against Canaris was flimsy, with no admission on his part and no physical evidence. It was more based on Hansen's say so and the fact that other suspected conspirators had shot themselves, which to the Gestapo was a case of guilty by association. It was only when Canaris's personal diary was discovered that the Gestapo felt that they finally had sufficient evidence to charge him with involvement in the 20 July plot against Hitler.

Canaris was held at Flossenbürg concentration camp, and it was there on 8 April 1945 that he faced what was known as a 'drumhead' court martial, or a court martial that is held 'in the field' to deal with urgent charges that relate to offences committed in action. No defence witnesses were allowed. The five men, including Canaris, who were on trial, were not even allowed to submit a defence and no record of the proceedings was kept. All of the men were found guilty of treason and sentenced to death. Canaris was hanged on 9 April at the Flossenbürg camp just two weeks before it was liberated by American forces. In a final act by the Nazis to strip Canaris of any dignity, he was made to strip before he went to the gallows.

The proceedings were initiated by SS General Ernst Kaltenbrunner who was the Chief of the Reich Main Security office.

General Erwin von Lahousen was a member of the *Abwehr*, as well as of the German resistance. He was also involved in the plots to assassinate Hitler of 13 March 1943 and 20 July 1944. He had supplied the bomb that had been used in the 13 March 1943 assassination plot. At the Nuremberg trials held between 20 November 1945 and 1 October 1946, he was a witness against Hermann Göring, along with twenty-one other Nazi defendants.

Hans Bernd Gisevius was an *Abwehr* intelligence officer and a German diplomat who worked in Zurich. He was a liaison officer between the station chief for America's Office of Strategic Services – or as they were more commonly referred to, OSS – and German Resistance forces in Germany. Both men, who worked under Canaris, gave further evidence at Nuremberg of his personal courage in attempting to oppose Hitler.

It would be somewhat ironic if the attempts made by Canaris and Wichmann to undermine Operation Sealion were actually a waste of time if Hitler had never actually intended for the operation to take place.

Chapter Six
Abwehr – German Military Intelligence

The *Abwehr*, or the German Military Intelligence service came into being in 1920, during the time of the *Reichswehr* and continued on into the time of the *Wehrmacht*, the names of the German Ministry of Defence between 1919 and 1945. This was despite Germany being prevented from establishing an intelligence organization by the restraints of the Treaty of Versailles. The initial purpose of the *Abwehr* was the prevention of foreign espionage on German soil. The remit of the organization changed greatly between the two wars, but in essence consisted of three main responsibilities: reconnaissance, cipher and radio monitoring and counter espionage. Up until 1929 the different German military services, had separate intelligence sections, but after that time they were centralised within the Ministry of Defence under the command of General Kurt Ferdinand Friedrich Hermann von Schleicher.

The *Abwehr* had offices throughout Germany, which were usually to be found anywhere there was an Army district, in territories that were under German occupation, as well as friendly 'neutral' countries.

In June 1932 Captain Konrad Patzig became the chief of the *Abwehr*, which was unusual because most of those who worked for the organization were in the main, army officers, yet Patzig was a naval officer. Having upset Hitler in 1934 by conducting aerial reconnaissance missions into Poland after he had signed a non-aggression treaty with them, Pantzig was fired from the *Abwehr* in January 1935, only to then become the man in charge of the *Admiral Graf Spee*, Germany's new pocket battleship. The man who took over from him at the *Abwehr* was Wilhelm Canaris, who began his new job on 1 January 1935. He was under no illusions as to how difficult his work would be. Patzig informed him of the problems he had with both Himmler and Reinhard Heydrich, who wanted all German intelligence organizations under their control to become part of the *Sicherheitsdienst des Reichsführers-SS*, more commonly referred to as the SD. This was the intelligence section of the SS and the Nazi Party and had been formed back in 1931. If they had been the single agency dealing with intelligence in Nazi Germany, the chances are they would not have shared any information with any branches of the military and would have more likely looked to gain control over the country's civilian population. At the Nuremberg trials, the SD was declared to be a criminal organization.

As was the norm in Nazi Germany, many of the senior Nazis spent a lot of their time vying for Hitler's attention and approval, which sometimes resulted in different agencies spending more time battling amongst themselves, so that they lost sight of what their real purpose actually was. The problem with having a nation's intelligence system split amongst different agencies, meant that there was a risk that the country would suffer. Intelligence was a very precious commodity, with the agency who discovered it quite often reluctant to share it with other internal agencies, even if it was relevant to them. To have control of incoming intelligence in Nazi Germany made the agency in possession of it, important and invaluable.

In 1935 the German Ministry of Defence became the Ministry of War, which in turn was replaced by the newly created *Oberkommando der Wehrmacht* in 1938, or as it was more commonly referred to, the OKW, which in English translated into the High Command of the Wehrmacht. But the *Abwehr* kept its role in military intelligence under the command of Vice-Admiral Wilhelm Canaris, working out of offices in the centre of Berlin.

In 1938 the *Abwehr* became three sections when Canaris decided it was time to re-organize his agency. There was the Central Division, the Foreign Branch and the *Abwehr*. The Central Division came under the command of General Hans Paul Oster, a close ally of Canaris. It was responsible for all financial dealings including the payments made to its agents. It also catered for all of the agency's personnel matters.

A large part of the work of the Foreign Branch, which later became the Foreign Intelligence Group, was connected to liaising with other elements of the German and Nazi authorities. This liaison often involved contact with the OKW and the general staffs of all branches of the German armed forces. It also discussed all on-going military matters with colleagues from the German Foreign Ministry. The most important aspect of its work was the evaluation of any and all captured enemy documents, along with determining the worth and importance that should be given to any foreign press releases and wireless broadcasts.

The main purpose of the *Abwehr* section was intelligence gathering, but it was sub-divided into a total of eighteen separate departments. When the numerous areas that they covered are considered, it makes it even harder to understand how their agents were so badly trained, and why they performed so badly in the field. The only rational explanation is that the *Abwehr* handlers wanted them to be as bad as they were. Another aspect hard to believe is that the *Abwehr* had absolutely no idea that so many of their agents had been turned by British Military Intelligence. All of the information that the agents were passing back to their handlers appears to have been accepted without question. The best example of this was the information that they received telling them that the main Allied invasion force was going to come ashore at Calais, and that although there would be a diversionary landing on the beaches of Normandy, this was no more than a bluff.

It would appear that the *Abwehr* played a massive part in ensuring that Britain and her Allies defeated Nazi Germany, before the nation was ruined beyond repair.

The different departments within the *Abwehr* section included those that dealt with false documents, photos, penetration of foreign intelligence agencies, planting false information, acts of sabotage on German soil, inks and passports, intelligence from numerous locations throughout German occupied Europe. They were tasked with making direct contact with discontented minority groups in foreign countries, such as they did with the IRA in Ireland.

By the outbreak of war Canaris had long since not only become disenchanted with Hitler and the Nazi party, but he was extremely concerned about the direction in which they were taking the nation. Maybe he had a premonition of the terrors, death and destruction that were to follow, none of which would be beneficial for his country. Canaris surrounded himself with like-minded people, who felt as passionately as he did about saving Germany from the horrors of Nazism, people who he knew that he could trust. With his opposition to Hitler, he needed those around him whom he could trust; if he didn't have that, it could – and did – cost him his life.

Amongst his inner circle of hand-picked staff he had appointed General Rudolf Bamler as the man in charge of Section III, hoping that he would be able to gain the trust of Himmler. However, he was extremely selective about what operational information he allowed Bamler to have sight or knowledge of as he did not trust him. Hitler and the officers of his High Command had absolutely no idea of the threat from within their own ranks, because Canaris had men around him who were more loyal to him than they were to Nazi Germany, which was no mean feat.

The *Abwehr* had been liaising with the Irish Republican Army (IRA) since 1937, a 'relationship' which continued through until 1944 when it became clear that defeat for Hitler and his Allies was just a matter of time. The main purpose of the connection between the two was the potential help it could provide the Nazis in any future invasion of Britain. Nazi Germany and the *Abwehr* were well aware of the IRA's political and para-military struggle with the British Government, and their ultimate desire to separate Northern Ireland from the United Kingdom.

The Second World War was always a case of when rather than if. War had been the intention of Hitler and Nazi Germany from as soon as they gained power in 1933; all they were waiting for was the right moment when, as a nation, Hitler felt that they were strong enough to succeed. During the six years between coming to political prominence and the beginning of the Second World War, Hitler didn't waste his time. It was the gathering of such intelligence that ultimately helped him make many of his decisions. But until Canaris's reorganization of the *Abwehr* in 1938, it had not been renowned as being a particularly professional unit, which was not reflective of the ethos and reputation of the rest of Hitler's Nazi Germany.

In the summer of 1936 Hitler sent Canaris to Madrid as a special envoy to try and persuade Franco to join with Germany in the coming war against Britain. Gibraltar had strategic importance and could be of great value to Germany in the event of war. But despite the instructions given to him by Hitler, this is not what Canaris did. Instead he advised Franco that he would be much better off staying out of the fight as he was almost certain that the war was going to end in disaster for Germany. By advising Franco not to take sides with Germany, Canaris was taking a massive risk, because if Franco told Hitler what his special envoy had advised him to do, it would have meant certain death for Canaris. To try and covertly undermine the Nazi regime under which he served in this way was proof, if it were needed, of his determination to bring about the defeat and downfall of Hitler and the Nazi party, regardless of the personal cost.

Canaris reported back to Hitler that Franco would not commit Spanish forces in an alliance with him, until Britain had been defeated. Other than supposition, it is difficult to know for certain the exact conversation which took place between the two men, as what they said and discussed was not recorded, maybe because both men knew full well the danger they would be in if an actual record of their meeting had been kept and subsequently came to light. A point worth noting though is the Spanish government were keen to display their gratitude to Canaris and later did this in the form of providing a pension to Canaris's widow, at the end of the Second World War. The question is, why?

Paul Thummel was a high-ranking member of the *Abwehr* and a highly decorated member of the Nazi Party. He was also a double agent who spied for Czechoslovakia. In March 1937 he passed on information about Germany's intelligence services to members of Czechoslovakia's security services, who in turn forwarded it to the Secret Intelligence Service in London. The information he provided was absolutely staggering. It included detailed information of Germany's intelligence system, her overall military capabilities and intentions, the complete order of battle of both the Wehrmacht and the Luftwaffe, along with her mobilisation plans. What was even more remarkable was that he provided the Allies with warnings of Germany's intended annexation of the Sudetenland, along with the invasions of Poland and Czechoslovakia. Despite this information being provided in 1937, the events that they related to still went ahead some two years later.

Thummel's treachery was finally discovered by the Nazis and he was executed by the SS at the Theresienstadt concentration camp in April 1945. The camp was liberated by Russian forces on 8 May 1945.

Despite his growing concern about the direction in which Hitler was taking Germany, Canaris and his colleagues at the *Abwehr* continued with their work on the planned invasion and annexation of neighbouring Austria, which took place in March 1938. This escalation of German land grabbing continued in October 1938, when Hitler sent his forces into the disputed Sudetenland.

By now a number of high-ranking German officers, along with some of those who worked for the German Foreign Office, were becoming increasingly concerned with the cavalier manner in which Hitler was behaving. They were concerned that his actions could result in another war in Europe, the first one having only finished just twenty years earlier, and which ended catastrophically for Germany and her people. It was with these very same fears in mind that a group of like-minded individuals, including Canaris, General Erwin von Witzleben and Helmuth Groscurth, formed a group to try and help Germany from being led to extinction by a group of murdering, demented, psychopaths.

Von Witzleben was executed by the Nazis on 8 August 1944, for his part in the 20 July assassination plot against Adolf Hitler. As for Groscurth, he participated in the Battle of Stalingrad, where he helped draft the final message sent from the German forces trapped there. After the surrender he contracted typhus and died on 7 April 1943 whilst in Soviet captivity.

Canaris for his part attempted to open up lines of communication with British authorities, so concerned was he of the imminence of a European war. Before German forces carried out their invasion of Poland, the *Abwehr* even sent a special emissary, Ewald von Kleist-Schmenzin to London to warn the British authorities in person. Once again, an extremely brave, yet dangerous act by both Canaris and Kleist, as if news of this meeting had found its way back to Hitler, it would have meant certain death for them both.

Kleist was an officer in the Wehrmacht during the Second World War, and his parents were active in the German resistance. Kleist, aged 22, was designated to kill Hitler in a suicide attack in January 1944, which did not take place due to Hitler changing his movements at the last moment. He was also the last surviving member of the group involved in the 20 July plot to assassinate Hitler.

Somewhat ironically, it was Canaris, on the direct orders of Adolf Hitler, who provided the Polish uniforms and small arms for German forces to carry out an attack on a German radio station whilst dressed as Polish soldiers. It was this staged and pretend attack which Hitler put great store by to use as justification for his invasion of Poland.

In the early years of the war the *Abwehr* proved to be quite an effective organization under the leadership of Canaris, especially during the early months of the war in what is often referred to as the Phoney War, the period between the outbreak of war on 3 September 1939 and the German invasion of France on 10 May 1940. It had a success with Operation North Pole which was a counter-intelligence operation of the *Abwehr*. German forces captured a number of Allied resistance agents who were operating in Holland and used their codes to trick the Allies into continuing to provide the agents with information and supplies. In all some fifty Allied agents were identified, captured and executed.

The *Abwehr* had agents in both Norway and Denmark who observed the arrivals and departures of all shipping that passed in and out of Danish and Norwegian ports. They forwarded this information on to the German military, especially the Luftwaffe, which resulted in the loss of more than 150,000 tons of Allied shipping.

Abwehr agents proved their worth in the build-up to Germany's invasion of neutral Norway on 9 April 1940, as they had been able to establish the strength and location of all Norwegian ground forces. This information not only greatly helped during the actual invasion, but also ensured that the Norwegians' defence would not be able to last for any protracted period of time. The fighting finished on 10 June 1940, when the final Norwegian forces surrendered. Norway remained under German occupation until all German forces surrendered to the Allies on 8/9 May 1945. It would be fair to say that in relation to the success of the invasion of Norway, the *Abwehr* had proved themselves to be an invaluable asset as part of the German military machine.

Hitler did not have any real desire to conquer Ireland, to occupy it, or to add it to his ever-increasing empire. The plan to invade Ireland was more of a diversionary tactic than anything else. Germany's main worry as far as Ireland was concerned was that she didn't side with Northern Ireland and Great Britain against Germany in any future invasion of Great Britain. Hitler had even gone as far as having an operational order drawn up for invading Ireland, Operation Green.

Despite its detailed nature, Operation Green was not conceived or intended to have been acted upon in an actual military sense. It was more to do with how matters would be perceived on the political stage, if it were known that there was an operation in place ready to be used. It certainly had the desired effect, and resulted in the British Government liaising with the government of the Irish Free State and coming up with an agreement that in the event of a German invasion of Ireland, British Armed Forces would occupy the country, in an effort to prevent such an invasion from taking place and to secure her neutrality.

Operation Green is sometimes confused with a similar operation, entitled Plan Kathleen, that was the brainchild of the Irish Republican Army (IRA), which they sent to the *Abwehr* in August 1940. But for Hitler, once he had given up on Operation Sealion and the invasion of Britain, there was very little or no need for any of his forces to occupy Ireland.

The involvement of the *Abwehr* with the IRA had different elements to it. The two organizations had been in cahoots with each other since before the outbreak of the war, but it could be regarded as a 'what if' relationship as the main reason for it was more as a precaution or a back-up should Germany ever decide she was going to invade mainland Britain. Other than that, there was no purpose to their relationship. The initial reason Germany had made contact and then looked to cultivate the relationship further, was because she knew that the IRA was against the British Government and wanted them out so that once again there could be a united Ireland.

Despite their eight-year association it was always going to be a somewhat difficult relationship. The IRA was not subordinate to the *Abwehr*, so the longer the relationship endured, the more it became about intelligence gathering of a kind that might be useful to the Nazis.

Hermann Görtz who was an agent of the *Abwehr* and a liaison officer between them and the IRA appears earlier in the book but the other *Abwehr* agent to fulfil that role was Ernst Weber-Drohl. Born near Edelbach in Austria in 1879, he went on to become a professional wrestler and a performing strongman, with his work allowing him to travel regularly to both America and Ireland and providing him with an excellent knowledge and use of the English language. He knew Ireland like 'the back of his hand'. With his geographical knowledge of Ireland and his command of the English language, at the outbreak of the Second World War, he came to the attention of the *Abwehr* in Nuremberg.

After undergoing and completing his training, he was tasked with making a delivery to the IRA. His contact was Seamus O'Donovan in Dublin. On 8 February 1940, Weber-Drohl was dropped off on the Irish coast at Killala, by the German submarine *U-37* and began making his way to shore in a rubber dingy. He had with him documentation, money and a radio transmitter, all of which he had been instructed to deliver to his contact in the IRA. Unfortunately for him, the sea was rough and his dingy capsized, causing the radio transmitter to be lost. He made it ashore and met up with his contact, handing over an undisclosed sum of money and the surviving documentation.

The *U-37* was a very successful German submarine and between October 1939 and March 1940, was responsible for sinking a total of fifty-five Allied merchant and naval vessels.

On 24 April 1940, after having been at large for just over eight weeks, Weber-Drohl was arrested in Ireland for illegally entering the country, but for some reason he was set free by the district court. His freedom was extremely short lived, however, and he was immediately re-arrested under the Emergency Powers Act and incarcerated. His response was to go on hunger strike, and after just eight days, he was released from custody. He was re-arrested in 1942 and spent the rest of the war in a combination of Mountjoy Prison, in Phibsborough, Dublin, and Athlone internment camp in Leinster, where he was held with other German agents. It is interesting to note that because he was in Ireland when he was arrested, Weber-Drohl's actions saw him being interned for the rest of the war. If he had been detained in Britain, he would have no doubt been tried in a criminal court, found guilty and hanged.

The *Abwehr* came up with numerous different operations throughout the war on how best to infiltrate their agents into Great Britain.

Operation Lobster

This was dated 1940, the intention being for German agents to be infiltrated into Britain and Ireland from Northern France and Norway. After Germany's victory in France, the *Abwehr* were tasked with obtaining information about British defences including the viability of German forces landing in Ireland and the creation and insertion of a fifth column into Britain which could perform sabotage and join up with invading German ground troops.

Abwehr II's diary for 25 June 1940, included the following:

> On the direction of the Head of Division (Lahousen Generalmajor Erwin von Lahousen) Abwehr II's work has in the main been switched over to the war with England. In addition, preparations are being made for work overseas. The only work in the east now concerns looking after the Ukrainian minority and transferring old contacts to Abwehr III. At the same time Abwehr II's work in Holland, Belgium and France is diminishing and being transferred.

Operation Lobster was connected to Operation Sea Lion, in that Lobster was put in place to see if the latter was a viable option.

Operation lobster 1

This was another *Abwehr* plan to infiltrate three German spies into Ireland in July 1940.

Operation Seagull (Ireland)

This was a mission sanctioned by the *Abwehr II* and the Brandenburg Regiment, that was launched in September 1940. The purpose of the operation was to infiltrate the UK as part of the preparation for Operation Sealion. Although the operation was actually launched, it was aborted during the sea crossing to Ireland. This happened despite *Abwehr* Chief Wilhelm Canaris having issued orders that the *Abwehr* were not try and make any attempts to infiltrate agents into Britain or Ireland for the foreseeable future, because of the total failure of Operation Lobster 1. The problem arose because Operation Seagull had been under the command of the German Army Group Northern France/Belgium, and not the *Abwehr*.

Operation Seagull 1

This was an *Abwehr II* sanctioned mission in May 1942. The plan was for an *Abwehr* agent to sabotage the power station at Fort William in Scotland. The agent chosen for the mission was an Irish prisoner of war. He was to be parachuted into the Glasgow area where he would meet up with two Irishmen. There were actually two designated targets, the electric power station at Fort William and the hydroelectric production facility at Kinlochleven. In June 1942 this was changed so that it was carried out at the same time as Operation Seagull 2 in Ireland, with both teams communicating by radio.

The planning for Seagull 1 began in earnest after Operation Innkeeper had failed miserably. The Germans had recruited a number of Irish prisoners of war from camps in Germany and Poland. The agent chosen by the Germans for this mission was Irishman Andrew Walsh, who was also known by the code name of 'Vickers'. He had served with the British Expeditionary Force, and was more than likely captured at Dunkirk in May 1940.

Following the completion of their training, Walsh, who was going on Seagull 1 and James Brady who had been allocated to Seagull 2, were due to be flown to Norway, but just before take-off, a message was received that Norway was no longer their destination. Instead they had been ordered to fly to Berlin. The reason for this sudden and late change, was because it had come to the attention of the *Abwehr* command that Walsh had told a fellow prisoner-of-war, Harry Cushing, that on arriving in Britain, he didn't intend going ahead with the mission, but instead he was going to hand himself in to the local police. Both men were arrested and Operation Seagull 1, was cancelled permanently.

Operation Seagull 2

The plan was to use an Irish *Abwehr* agent who would parachute into the area south-east of Ballycastle in Northern Ireland. Once there he would recruit a sabotage team made up of IRA members and attack important 'targets of opportunity' in the immediate vicinity. The two operations had been intended to take place simultaneously with the help of radio transmissions, but this all changed once Operation Seagull 1 had been cancelled permanently.

Operation Whale

This was name of two separate German plans conceived in 1940. Operation Walfisch and Operation Wal. Walfisch was a plan to land a seaplane on a lake in Ireland, but never took place and was abandoned. Wal was a plan devised in November 1940, to make contact with both Scottish and Welsh nationalist groups in readiness for the German invasion of Britain. The operation never took place and was abandoned in April 1941.

Operation Dove (Ireland)

This is also sometimes known as Operation Pigeon. It was a mission devised in early 1940. The idea was to transport two members of the IRA, who had been in Berlin, to Ireland. Both men left from Wilhelmshaven on board the German submarine *U-65* on the evening of 8 August 1940. During the journey, one of the men was taken ill, complaining of severe stomach pains. There was no doctor on board the submarine and he died on 14 August and was buried at sea.

Operation Sea Eagle

This is sometimes referred to as Operation Dove 2, and was a plan conceived by the German Foreign Ministry in May 1941 after the collapse of Operation Whale. The operation was to involve landing a seaplane on a lake in Ireland to supply funds and a transmitter to the IRA. The reason for this was because of German fears that American forces who were soon to be stationed in Northern Ireland would be used for an invasion of Ireland. Operation Sea Eagle never took place.

Plan Kathleen

This is sometimes referred to as Artus Plan and was a plan for an amphibious invasion of Northern Ireland by German forces, consisting of 50,000 troops, in the vicinity of Derry. Details of the planned operation were discovered during a raid on a house in Ireland. A copy of it was sent by the Garda to MI5 in London, who in turn sent a copy of it on to the Royal Ulster Constabulary in Belfast. The plan was never acted upon and had been drawn up as an operation to be undertaken as part of Hitler's planned invasion of mainland Britain, which of course never took place.

Operation Mainau

This was a German espionage mission. It was sanctioned and planned by the *Abwehr* and successfully took place in May 1940. The mission was quite simple. It involved the insertion of *Abwehr* agent Hermann Görtz into Ireland by parachute. He was tasked with:

1. Establishing a secure communications link between Ireland and Germany.
2. To consult the IRA on the prospect of a reconciliation between the Irish state and the IRA.
3. Direct the military activities of the IRA towards British military targets, specifically naval installations.
4. Report any incidental items of military importance.

The attempt to insert him into Ireland was originally planned to take place in April but this was cancelled due to bad weather. It eventually went ahead on the night of 4 May 1940.

Operation Innkeeper

This was an aborted plan drawn up in Autumn 1941 to send two Irish *Abwehr* agents to London on a sabotage mission. One of the agents was a John Codd, an Irish national captured while serving as a soldier in the British Army in 1940. The mission never took place.

Operation Osprey

This was a plan drawn up by the German Foreign Ministry and *Abwehr* II during 1942. In essence the plan was a re-vamp of Operation Whale. Planning for the operation was driven by the landing of a small contingent of 4,508 American troops and engineers in Northern Ireland on 26 January 1942, and Hitler's fears about what this could lead to. A small Waffen-SS unit was to be parachuted into Ireland to support any local parties who were prepared to take on the Americans. The Waffen-SS unit or the operation, were never put to the test in Ireland because the American invasion of Ireland, which German High Command felt might take place, never occurred.

The Western Desert Campaign of 1941-42 was a good example of how effective the use of intelligence could be. Sometimes this was because of accurate information and on other occasions it was because misinformation had been believed.

In North Africa the British conducted an operation of deception. It began when the *Abwehr* recruited an Italian of Jewish heritage in France during 1940. What they didn't know was that he was a double agent who had been recruited by the British SIS before the war and who had given him the somewhat unusual code name of 'Cheese'.

The *Abwehr* sent him to Egypt in February 1941. His mission was to report on British military operations in the region. What he sent to his handlers back in Germany, by way of a fictitious sub-agent named Paul Nicosoff, were a number of prepared and doctored messages, which were sent to help the success of Operation Torch, which took place between 8 and 16 November 1942. It was the Anglo-American invasion of French North Africa. When it finally took place, it was a total surprise to the German High Command, showing just how effective the British deception had been.

North Africa became a hot bed for spies from all sides. The *Abwehr* went about obtaining people to spy for them in something of a strange manner. They approached Arab prisoners of war who were being held in French camps. This wasn't the first time the *Abwehr* had decided upon such an approach, they had employed a similar tactic with Soviet Union prisoners of war when they invaded Russia. They thought of it as being creative, but it appears more a case of desperation. They promised any Arab prisoners of war who agreed to spy for them in North Africa, a trip back to their homeland. Many, if not all, of those approached would have accepted the offer, but how many would have returned home from their break?

Major Witilo von Griesheim set up a network of German spies and wireless stations in Libya in early 1941, the purpose of which was to collect intelligence from the surrounding French territories. Just a few months later in July 1941, Admiral Canaris instructed Major Nikolas Ritter, a Luftwaffe officer who worked for him as part of the *Abwehr* I Section, to set up a unit in Egypt who had to covertly make their way into the country via the Libyan desert. He was accompanied by Laszlo Almasay, a Hungarian aristocrat, aviator and desert explorer, and their mission was to gather intelligence about the British-occupied country.

Ritter was injured in a crash landing and had to be extricated back to Germany for medical treatment, but instead of command of the group being given to a soldier, it was given to Laszlo Almasay. As part of Operation Salam, Almasay transported two of his German agents across the Libyan desert and behind enemy lines in Egypt. It was not a covert operation with Almasay and his men wearing German uniforms, although they were using captured British Ford cars and trucks, which were adorned with German military crosses.

The two German agents, Johannes Eppler and his radio operator Hans-Gerd Sandstede, were dropped off in the Egyptian town of Asyut, and Almasy and his team made it back to their base at Gialo in Libya unhindered. What Almasy didn't know, nor the German command for that matter, was that the cipher Almasy and his agents used for their wireless transmissions had been compromised. It had been broken by British code breakers at Bletchley Park in England.

Eppler and Sandstede made their way to Cairo after having been dropped at Asyut, but were captured less than six weeks after arriving there. For Almasy, it was a bittersweet experience. For delivering Eppler and Sandstede to Asyut, he was awarded the Iron Cross and promoted to the rank of captain. With his services no longer required in North Africa, he returned to Hungary.

A special unit, the Sonderkommando Dora, which was under the command of *Abwehr* officer Oberstleutnant Walter Eichler, was set up in January 1942. Its members included cartographers, geologists and mineralogists, and their job was to study desert topography and assess the suitability of desert terrain for military purposes. By November the same year, and with German and other Axis forces in full retreat from El Alamein, there was no more use for Eichler's unit and they were withdrawn from North Africa.

The *Abwehr* recruited an Iranian national in Hamburg before the outbreak of the war, but unknown to the Germans he was turned into a double agent by a joint team of British and Russian intelligence officers, who allocated him the code name 'Kiss'. He was based at the intelligence centre in Baghdad and from late 1944 he provided the *Abwehr* with a stream of false information on the movement of British and Russian troop movements throughout Iraq and Iran, which was provided by his Allied controllers.

There are numerous accounts of how anti-Nazi the *Abwehr* were, but equally there were reports of some of their operatives being pro-Nazi. The truth is, it was a combination of both. The SS certainly had their suspicions about where their loyalties lay, as did Adolf Hitler. The SS, on more than one occasion, placed *Abwehr* officers under investigation and certainly had them closely monitored, suspecting them of being involved in assassination plots against Hitler.

An incident took place at Wieblingen near Heidelberg in Germany on 10 September 1943, which subsequently resulted in the dissolution of the *Abwehr*. The incident in question was known as the 'Frau Solf Tea Party'. The party was given by Elizabeth von Thadden, a Protestant headmistress of a famous girls' school. The widow of Dr Wilhelm Solf, who was a former Colonial Minister and an ex-ambassador to Japan, under Kaiser Wilhelm II, Frau Johanna Solf had long been involved in the anti-Nazi intellectual movement that existed in Berlin.

Von Thadden brought with her an attractive young man, a Swiss doctor by the name of Paul Reckzeh, who supposedly worked at the

Charité Hospital in Berlin under Professor Ferdinand Sauerbruch. He was polite, well-mannered and made a favourable impression on the other members of the group who were at the tea party. As was common amongst the Swiss, Reckzeh expressed anti-Nazi sentiments during the conversations, and offered to convey letters of those present to their friends in Switzerland, an offer that many accepted. What they didn't know was that Dr Reckzeh was in fact a Gestapo agent. When he returned to his office after the tea party, he wrote a report about who was there, what each of them said, what they were discussing, and handed over the letters to his bosses which he been given by most of those who had been present. On 12 January 1944 everybody who had been at the party, except Frau Solf and her daughter, Countess Lagi Grafin von Ballestrem, were arrested and later executed. This resulted in seventy-four people losing their lives.

Those at the party included Otto Kiep, an official from the German Foreign Office; Countess Hannah von Bredow, the granddaughter of Otto von Bismarck; Count Albrecht von Bernstoff, the nephew of Count Johann Heinrich von Bernstorff, the German ambassador to the United States during the First World War; Father Friedrich Erxleben, a well-known Jesuit priest and Nokolaus von Halem, a successful merchant. In June 1944, shortly before the 20 July 1944 assassination attempt on Adolf Hitler, von Halem appeared before the People's Court when he was indicted for conspiracy to commit treason and for undermining the war effort. He was found guilty as charged and sentenced to death. He was executed by guillotine in Brandenburg-Görden Prison on 9 October 1944. Richard Kuenzer, a legation adviser, was executed on 23 April 1945 for his part in the 20 July plot. After having been arrested by the Gestapo, Arthur Zarden committed suicide on 18 January 1945, knowing he was likely to be tortured. His daughter Irmgard Zarden was arrested on suspicion of being involved in the same plot, but was aquitted due to lack of evidence and released in July 1945.

The German Air Ministry had tapped a number of telephone conversations between Reckzeh and the Gestapo about the anti-Nazi intellectual movement. A member of staff who worked in the Air Ministry was a friend of Helmuth James Graf von Melke and told him that he and other members of the movement had been named in the tapped phoned conversations.

The Solfs managed to escape and made it to Bavaria but were eventually discovered by the Gestapo and were sent to the Ravensbrück concentration camp. It was around about this time that both Otto Kiep and Moltke were also arrested by the Gestapo.

One of Kiep's closest friends was Erich Vemehren, a lawyer by profession but during the Second World War, he became a member of the *Abwehr* in the Istanbul branch in Turkey, where he lived with his wife. His entire family had been anti-Nazi and in 1938 he refused to join the Hitler Youth movement and, because of a childhood injury, he was also excluded from having to undertake wartime military service.

Soon after Kiep's arrest the Vemehrens were requested to return to Berlin by the Gestapo, where they were to be interrogated about their friendship and connection with Kiep. Guessing that their homecoming wasn't going to be a pleasant experience, rather than returning to Berlin as they had been requested to do, in February 1944 they decided to get in touch with the British Secret Intelligence Service, who were interested in what they had to say. Time was of the essence. If the Gestapo became aware of what the Vemehrens were up to, their lives would have been in serious danger. They were quickly flown to Cairo and from there to England.

Once the British Secret Intelligence Service had the Vemehrens safely back in England, they wasted no time in letting the world know of their defection; it certainly reached the ears of the German authorities in Berlin, especially those of the Gestapo. Understandably, they were not happy, especially as it was believed that the Vemehrens had taken the *Abwehr*'s secret codes with them which they handed them over to the British.

The issues surrounding the 'Solf Circle' and the defections of the Vemehrens, had somewhat of a dramatic outcome for the *Abwehr*, because as far as Adolf Hitler was concerned, not only was it the last straw, but it was damning evidence that showed that the *Abwehr* had somehow been infiltrated by Allied agents. On 18 February 1944 Hitler ordered that the organization should be disbanded and its work taken over by the *Reichssicherheitshauptamt* or RSHA, which answered to Heinrich Himmler. Many of the original *Abwehr* officers resigned rather than having to work for the SS.

Kiep was severely tortured while in detention, and once the Gestapo finally acquired confirmation of his involvement in the 20 July plot to assassinate Hitler, he was executed at Plötzensee Prison in Berlin on 15 August 1944 where the method of despatching somebody to the after-life was mainly by the use of 'Madame Guillotine'. The same fate befell Elizabeth von Thadden who was executed on 8 September 1944.

Arthur Zarden was appointed as State Secretary in June 1932, but a problem would soon arise as Zarden was married to a Jewish woman and had himself become a follower of the Jewish faith. Once Hitler and the Nazis came to power in 1933, Hitler had him thrown out of office forcing him into what was known as provincial retirement on 31 March 1933. Under the Law for the Restoration of the Professional Civil Service, that retirement became permanent at the end of that year. After being arrested by the Gestapo on 12 January 1944, Zarden's fear of being tortured grew and grew. On 18 January, possibly fearing he would talk under torture and not wanting to name or implicate any of his friends and co-conspirators, he jumped from a window high up in the prison, falling to his death in the street below.

Zarden's daughter, Irmgard, was also arrested in the Gestapo purge of looking for those responsible and involved in the 20 July Plot. She spent five months incarcerated at Ravensbrück concentration camp, before being released due to a lack of evidence and no admission of guilt on her part.

Bernstorff and Solf were repeatedly tortured by the Gestapo in an effort to get them to talk about their part in the 20 July Plot. They too were held at Ravensbrück camp but were not there when the camp was liberated by the Russians on 25 April 1945. It is believed that along with Richard Kuenzer, Bernstorff was removed from Ravensbrück two days before it was liberated. His exact fate is unknown.

Nikolaus von Halem was arrested by the Gestapo on 26 February 1942 and spent time in a number of prisons and concentration camps. In June 1944 he was indicted for conspiracy to commit treason and for undermining the war effort. He was found guilty, sentenced to death and hanged on 9 October 1944.

Frau Johanna Solf and her daughter were arrested and interned at the Ravensbrück concentration camp, before being transferred to the Moabit Remand Prison in December 1944 while awaiting a trial which was to never take place. This was in part due to the intervention of the Japanese ambassador, Hiroshi Oshima, who knew the Solfs, and was also unwittingly a major source of communications intelligence for the Allies. Their trial was further delayed because the prosecution file of 'evidence' against them was destroyed as a result of an Allied air raid on 3 February 1945. They were released from prison on 23 April 1945 as the Russians entered Berlin.

Because of the connection between a large number of *Abwehr* personnel being involved in the 20 July Plot to assassinate him, Hitler fired Canaris and on 18 February 1944, he signed the document that abolished the *Abwehr*, with Canaris being given the title of Chief of the Office of Commercial and Economic Warfare, although it is unclear if such a position had ever previously existed in Nazi Germany. He was arrested on 23 July 1944, in the immediate aftermath of the July 20 assassination plot. Along with his deputy Oyster, Canaris was executed before the end of the war.

The Nazis committed many atrocities during the Second World War, crimes that at the end of the war, many of them had to answer for. Unfortunately for the Nazis, the *Abwehr* had assembled a secret dossier of the crimes and atrocities they had carried out in Eastern Europe. This dossier became known as the Zossen documents, with its intention to expose their crimes at an unspecified time in the future. The dossier was kept in a safe at the Zossen military headquarters.

There were a series of deep underground bunkers built south of Berlin, near Zossen, Brandenburg. Their purpose was to house the High Command of the Germany Army and the Supreme Command of the Armed Forces. Wehrmacht field operations were also planned at that location, as well as being a connection between Berlin's military and civilian authorities. The dossier was eventually discovered by the Gestapo, handed over to Ernst Kaltenbrunner, the head of the SD, who took them with him to Schloss Mittersill in the Tyrol, Austria, where he burned them.

In the years after the war, history hasn't necessarily been kind to the *Abwehr*. They have been accused of being inept, having a poor image, being corrupt, inefficient and negligent. It is even said that some of the German Army's losses were down to the poor quality of the intelligence that the *Abwehr* produced. Some of these claims might well be true, but there doesn't seem to be any allowance or any acceptance that the *Abwehr* might have been doing these things intentionally. So aghast were they at the ever-increasing number of Nazi atrocities carried out in the name of their beloved Germany, that they wanted no part of it. By conducting themselves as they did, most of which was orchestrated by Canaris, they hoped to bring an end to Nazi Germany, and an end to the war before there was nothing left to save. They would rather the Allies were victorious, because at least that way it would finally mean an end to Nazism.

I believe that the Allied victory in the Second World War was in no small part down to the *Abwehr*. An organization such as theirs could simply have not made so many 'mistakes' unintentionally, leaving me with the belief that what they did, they did intentionally.

Chapter Seven

Undetected Spy – Engelbertus Fukken

Engelbertus Fukken was born in the Hague, Holland in 1914, at the beginning of the Great War. Aged 19 in 1933, he joined the Dutch National Socialist Movement, which was affiliated to the National Socialist Workers Party of Germany, otherwise known as the Nazi Party. In 1934 he got a job as an agent for an insurance company working out of the Hague, but just six months in to his new employment he was arrested for fraud after failing to pay his employer the sums of money he had collected from his clients. He was charged, found guilty and sentenced to three months imprisonment. After his release he managed to acquire a job as a journalist for the weekly *Noordwijker* newspaper, but in 1937, he was sent back to prison for six months for being in breach of his original sentence. This resulted in him being expelled from the Dutch National Socialist Movement and losing his job with the newspaper.

On 10 May 1940 Germany invaded Holland and the subsequent fighting lasted until the main Dutch forces surrendered on 14 May, although a small force in the province of Zeeland continued to resist the Wehrmacht until 17 May.

The invasion witnessed some of the earliest mass paratrooper drops of the war. They were to occupy tactically identified locations, such as airfields, to assist German infantry units as they advanced across the country and to immobilise Dutch forces. The Luftwaffe bombed the city of Rotterdam on 14 May 1940, with devastating effects. Much of the old historic city centre was destroyed, and some 900 people were killed, as well as tens of thousands more left homeless. With this in mind, the General Staff of the Dutch military, knowing they could not prevent German bombers from wreaking similar havoc on other Dutch cities, ordered their soldiers to lay down their weapons and cease fighting.

In the aftermath of the German invasion, Rittmeister Kurt Mirow, who was part of German Military Intelligence, arrived in Noordwijk on 25 July 1940 looking to recruit spies, to work for them mainly in England. On arriving in Noordwijk, Mirow went to see a friend of his, Dieter Tappenbeck, a dedicated Nazi who worked in one of their ministries in Berlin, but who was in Noordwijk at the time of Mirow's arrival. It was Tappenbeck who suggested to Mirow that he approach a schoolboy friend of his, Engelbertus Fukken. Mirow and Fukken met and Mirow asked him if he would be prepared to become a spy for Nazi Germany. Fukken was only too pleased to oblige, even going as far as coming up with the name of Jan Willem Ter Braak, Ter Braak being a well-known Dutch journalist who had written widely about the Nazis.

After having undergone his training to become a spy, probably in Germany, his *Abwehr* masters were happy that what they had seen of Ter Braak was of a sufficient standard to become one of their secret agents working undercover in England.

Fukken was 26 years of age when he was parachuted into England under cover of darkness on 1 November 1940. He landed in Haversham, a picturesque and tranquil Buckinghamshire village. Unlike many of his compatriots, Fukken decided not to bury his parachute once he had landed, which was not the brightest of things to have done as it was found a few days later. The reason why he was sent to England is unknown, although over the years speculation as to why he was sent has varied greatly. By the time his parachute had been discovered, Fukken had already arrived in the city of Cambridge, having walked all the way, a distance of about fifty miles. Once in Cambridge he found some lodgings with a local family by the name of Sennitt, who lived at 58 St Barnabas Road. They readily accepted his cover story that he had arrived in England as a result of the Dunkirk evacuations in May 1941, and that he worked for a Dutch newspaper in London as part of the Free Dutch Forces.

According to his false identity papers his name was Jan Wilhelm Ter Braak. Despite acceptance of his details and status, Mr Sennitt went into his local police station and informed them that they had a Dutch man lodging with them, but for some inexplicable reason this was never followed up, probably because of wartime commitments.

During the war any foreign nationals living in England had to report to their local police station and have their details recorded. Not surprisingly, this wasn't something that Fukken did and he slipped through the net. But not registering would ultimately turn out to have fatal consequences for him. Foreigners living in England during the war, even if only as refugees, were entitled to ration cards which were required by everybody to acquire food.

Fukken's routine saw him spend most of his days away from his lodgings, although he returned each day, always sleeping in his rented room at the Sennitts' home. Somewhat surprisingly, Fukken left his suitcase transmitter in his room, rather than at an office he rented in the centre of Cambridge.

He spent most of his time travelling to different nearby locations, as well as London, by both bus and train, to check out areas that had been bombed by the Luftwaffe. He would make notes of the damage he had seen and the state of the people, and report back to his handlers in Hamburg. Everything went well for about four months, including the fact that by then it must have been obvious to him that the British authorities did not know of his presence in the country; if they had, they certainly would not have let him roam free. He supported himself by using cash; he had brought a large amount with him, in both pounds and dollars.

He was even stopped by Police and produced a forged ration card but somehow managed to talk himself out of the situation without being arrested. He then chased up his *Abwehr* handlers in Germany, repeatedly asking them to extricate him, but his request fell on deaf ears. When that failed, he asked them to send him some more money and ration cards, but once again, the *Abwehr* didn't assist their beleaguered agent. The batteries on his transmitter had begun running low in December 1940, which meant that he had to resort to writing letters in special ink to his *Abwehr* handler in Hamburg.

Fukken would have known that he was in an extremely precarious position. Not only was he running out of money, but without a ration card, he couldn't obtain food. His mind would have been in a state of confusion, uncertain as to why the *Abwehr* were unwilling to help him, either by sending him money and ration cards, or by getting him out of there. He had nobody with whom to discuss his situation and his continued feeling of abandonment would have only fuelled his paranoia as he would have known that discovery and capture by the British authorities would have meant certain death.

As time went on, his options became fewer and fewer and as March 1941 was drawing to an end, Fukken's money was nearly all used up. He had used the English notes first and then changed his American dollars through a lodger who also stayed with the Sennitts, and who worked in a local bank. By the end of March he didn't even have enough money left to pay for that month's rent.

On 29 March he went to Cambridge railway station where he deposited a large case in the left luggage office. On 1 April 1941, four months after he had arrived in England, he was found dead by an electrician in a public air raid shelter at Christ's Pieces Park in Cambridge. Lying by his feet was a handgun and amongst the possessions found on his body were a forged identity card and a Dutch passport, both in the name of Ter Braak. He also had what was left his money, 1/9d, and a ticket for the case he had left in the left luggage office. When Police later went to collect the case, they discovered that it contained a radio transmitter.

The police found the address of his lodgings and on searching his room discovered he had left items of property and personal belongings, but nothing of significance in relation to his being a spy. They did find a photograph of a young woman which had the shop's address on it and forwarded this on to the Dutch authorities who in November 1946 found the woman in the photograph and informed her of his death. It was Fukken's fiancée, Neeltj van Roon. She never spoke of what happened to her fiancé.

The photograph of his dead body which appears on the Wikipedia website strikes me as being somewhat strange. Although I am neither a forensic pathologist nor a firearms expert, I do have ten years of firearms experience and begin with an assumption that the body hadn't been moved before the photograph was taken. For a start most people are right-handed but as the body is lying on its right side, he wasn't shot by a right-handed person. So that leaves a left-handed person but looking at the photograph that doesn't add up either. If somebody shot themselves in the head with a handgun they were holding in their left hand whilst in a standing position, the gun would instinctively move upwards and backwards meaning that it would more than likely fall somewhere behind him. As for his left arm, that just doesn't look like a natural position for it to be in after having shot himself in the head. There are two other points I would like to make. If Fukken was in such a depressed state of mind that he took his own life surely he would have just shot himself at his lodgings. Why go to all the effort of walking to a public air raid shelter and risk bumping into a police officer on the way. The final point is, during the Second World War Germany issued twenty-three different types of handguns to its units. I have not been able to identify the handgun lying on the ground in the photograph, as one of those twenty-three.

Did Fukken commit suicide? I don't know. Is it possible? Yes, but I do not believe the available information and photographic evidence prove that he did.

An inquest into Fukken's death was hastily arranged at the local coroner's office where it took place in secrecy. The findings were not released until after the war, on 8 September 1945. Members of MI5 decided that his body should be buried in an unmarked grave in the cemetery at the nearby village of Great Shelford.

Chapter Eight

Arthur Owens

Arthur Graham Owens was a Welshman born at Portardawe, Glamorgan in 1899, one of three children born to William Thomas and Ada Owens. The 1911 Welsh census shows Arthur and his parents living at 32 Grove Road, Portadawe, Glamorgan. William Owens, who by then was aged 66, was a retired plumber. In the years before the war Owens had a company that made commercial-sized batteries for the Royal Navy. He also had a similar contract with the German equivalent, the Kriegsmarine, in Kiel.

Arthur's first contact with the world of spying and espionage happened in 1936, when he was approached by the British Secret Intelligence Service to provide information for them about what he saw in the German shipyards.

In 1938 Owens, a fervent Welsh Nationalist, and no great lover of the English, or the rest of the United Kingdom for that matter, was approached by an *Abwehr* agent in Britain, Nikolaus Ritter, the Chief of Air Intelligence in German military intelligence, who led spy rings in the United States and Great Britain between 1936 to 1941.

In 1938 Owens visited Germany under the guise of his work, and whilst there, he was recruited by the *Abwehr*. Although the money he was paid by the Germans came in handy, it was the attractive young women the *Abwehr* provided to help quench his sexual appetite that he really liked. To go with the sex and money, the Germans gave him the code name of 'Johnny'.

When Owens returned to Britain, he decided to inform his contact at the British Secret Intelligence Service (MI6), of the German approach. Whether that was out of loyalty, unlikely as he was a Welsh Nationalist, or a fear of being discovered and unmasked as a German spy, is unclear. He also told his contact that he was soon to receive a radio transceiver from the Germans, which he did. The only confusion surrounds how he actually came by it. He went to Germany to collect it, although he told the British Secret Intelligence Service that it had been left for him at the left luggage office at Victoria railway station in London. This was in the early months of 1939. Owens handed the radio set over to the British and their experts for examination, and they were astounded to discover that it was far more advanced than the ones they had at the time.

Less than a month before the outbreak of the Second World War Owens was in Germany visiting his *Abwehr* controller at his office in Hamburg with his girlfriend. As the saying goes, 'hell hath no fury like a woman scorned' and this was most certainly the case as far as Owens was concerned. Despite being with his girlfriend, he was still a married man, although he and his wife were separated. Whilst he was in Germany a letter arrived at the *Abwehr* offices in Hamburg informing them that her husband was in fact a British spy. Not content with writing a letter to the Germans, she also informed the British police that he was spying for Germany. Not surprisingly, nothing was done by either side, and Owens simply walked back into the country on his return on 23 August 1939. My guess is that the British police informed the British security services, and were told to leave the matter well alone, although I doubt that they went in to too much detail, if any at all, about any connection between them and Owens – there was, after all, a war just about to begin.

September 1939 was an interesting time for Owens. The Second World War began on 1 September 1939, when Germany invaded Poland. Two days later on 3 September, Britain declared war on Germany, and six years of death, murder and destruction began. On 4 September, Owens offered his services to the Metropolitan Police's Special Branch, but the response he received wasn't what he was expecting. Instead of taking him up on his offer of assistance he was arrested and interned in Wandsworth Prison under Regulation 18B of the Defence (General) Regulations 1939. This allowed people suspected of being Nazi sympathisers to be detained without trial. It also suspended an individual's right to invoke *habeas corpus*, whereby an individual could report an unlawful detention or imprisonment and request that the court order the detained person to be brought before the court so that it could be determined if their detention was lawful.

In the meantime, MI6 had, unbeknown to Owens, been giving his situation some consideration. After having left Owens to stew in his cell at

Wandsworth Prison for eight days, they decided that he had the potential to make a good double agent. They took his transmitter to him in his prison cell, and in essence told him that he could either become a double agent for them or he could rot in his cell for the rest of the war. He agreed to work as a double agent. To start the ball rolling, personnel from MI6 and a prison warder watched over him whilst he tried to communicate with his *Abwehr* contacts in Germany.

He was released from Wandsworth Prison and put up in a large property with his German-issued transmitter radio and his girlfriend. Within a matter of days he had made his way to Rotterdam in Holland where he met with agents from the *Abwehr*. He gave them information about Britain's Chain Home, the code name for the ring of coastal early warning radar stations built by the Royal Air Force before and during the Second World War to detect and track aircraft. The radar units themselves were also known as Chain Home and it was the first early warning radar network in the world. Its effect on the outcome of the war made it one of Britain's most powerful weapons. In return the German agents asked him if it would be possible to poison water reservoirs in England.

For the information about the Chain Home system, the Germans paid Owens £470, which today would be enough to purchase a three bedroomed house.

In the early months of the war all that the Germans asked of Owen was to provide them with weather reports, which would be of use to the Luftwaffe. Providing this information also boosted his credibility with his German handlers. He was later instructed by them to start up a postage stamp business, so that they could communicate freely with him.

In December 1939, a further meeting took place in Brussels when *Abwehr*'s Nikolaus Ritter informed Owens that he would be sent a new and more powerful radio to send his messages, along with explosives. He was also given a large sum of money and was promised a monthly salary of £250 which at today's rates was a staggering £13,880. On his return to the UK he informed MI5 that what had been termed the Phoney War would come to an abrupt end in May 1940, information which proved to be very accurate.

Owens was anything but predictable, which made MI5 extremely suspicious of him and unsure as to how far they could actually trust him. This uncertainty wasn't helped when he chartered a Grimsby trawler to meet with Ritter on the Dogger Bank, some 140 miles out into the North Sea. With Owens was a second double agent, by the name of Samuel McCarthy, code name 'Biscuit', who had been put in place to test Owens' real intentions. The interesting aspect of this proposed meeting was that Ritter was due to arrive in a flying boat, specifically designed to be able to land on the water. The meeting never took place as Owens' chartered trawler and Ritter's flying boat couldn't locate each other. This turned out to be a massive let off for the British Security Services as Owens was found to have in his possession a complete list of all MI5's key personnel as of 1939. If that list had fallen into German hands, the outcome for the UK could have been catastrophic. MI6 were understandably livid at his potential betrayal. Owens was arrested and threatened with being executed for treason.

Whether he knew it or not, Owens was playing an extremely dangerous game, as neither the *Abwehr* nor MI5 totally trusted him. Each of those two organizations had to make the decision as to whether they persevered with him, or simply put a bullet through the back of his head and dispose of his body.

For MI5's part they had long since come to the conclusion that Owens was just interested in the money and how much he could make before the war ended. They decided to continue to use him, but in two ways. Firstly, they monitored his transmissions as best they could, so that he only passed on the information that they wanted him to. Secondly, they had a man by the name of Maurice Burton send messages that were purported to come from Owens. Burton had been the warder tasked with 'looking after him' during his time spent in Wandsworth Prison. He had observed so many of Owens' transmissions that he was able to mimic his style to a more than acceptable standard where the Germans would be happy that it was actually Owens sending the messages. What was ironic looking back on those times through today's eyes, is that there would have been a period of time when Owens was undoubtedly sending misinformation both to the British and the Germans.

The event which brought an end to Owens' life as a double agent took place in February 1941. MI5 allowed Owens to fly to neutral Portugal to once again meet with Ritter. On the trip Owens was accompanied by ex-Royal Naval Air Service officer, and fellow double agent, Walter Dicketts, who had the code name of 'Celery', and had worked in Air Intelligence during the First World War, but who then went on to serve numerous prison sentences for fraud. Unbeknown to Owens, Dicketts had been instructed by MI5 to take proof of his First World War staff appointment with him to prove his worth to the Germans. His mission was to convince the Germans he was a traitor who was willing to sell out his country in return for cash, whilst continuing to work for MI5. The other aspect of this mission was that MI5 needed a ready-made replacement for Owens if it ever got to the stage where they had no option but to dispense with his services.

Ritter listened to what Dicketts had to say, but the world of espionage could not survive by blind belief alone. Just because Dicketts had turned up in Lisbon and told Ritter that he was prepared to sell his country for money, that claim was never going to be accepted at face value, and Dicketts and MI6 both knew that. Ritter was up front with Dicketts and told him that before he could accept his story he would have to travel with him to Hamburg and agree to be interrogated by some of his colleagues. Dicketts had no choice but to agree.

Dicketts was now in unchartered waters and potentially in very grave danger, because if as a result of the interrogation Ritter and his colleagues were not convinced of his intentions, it could well cost him his life. Luckily for Dicketts his story was believed and he passed the interrogation.

Ritter gave Dicketts his first mission, which was on his return to England to purchase a boat so that he could collect other German agents and their equipment from the Nazi occupied Channel Islands and bring them to England.

Dicketts was in Hamburg for three weeks before he returned to Lisbon to be re-united with Owens, who had not been allowed by Ritter to travel with them to Hamburg. Soon after, Dicketts and Owens flew back home, but when they arrived in England the plot thickened. To start with Owens was discovered to be in possession of £10,000, more than half a million pounds by today's equivalent, as well as a number of explosive pens, neither of which he offered up. Maybe in an effort to lessen the consequences of being discovered with the money and explosives, Owens then claimed that on the way to Lisbon he told Dicketts that he had already informed Ritter that both of them were working for MI5. As if to give credence to his claim, he quoted Dicketts' willingness to go to Germany as proof that he had been turned by Ritter. Dicketts strenuously denied the allegation, but despite this MI5 still did not know who to believe. By the very nature of what these men did, they were excellent liars; they needed to be as in any given situation, their lives could depend on it.

Both men were strenuously interrogated and questioned for hours, and afterwards more of the MI5 interviewers believed Dicketts than they did Owens, but not all of them. The outcome of the affair was that Owens ended up in Dartmoor prison, where he remained until the end of the war, for having endangered Dicketts' life and for having informed Ritter that his pre-war radio transmitter was actually operated by MI5 and not him.

Owens' time at Dartmoor was spent in the hospital wing where all the internees were kept for their own protection rather than having them in general circulation with the other prisoners. This allowed Owens to continue to work for MI5 by befriending German internees and feeding back anything worthwhile he learned. On his release from prison in 1945, Owens signed the Official Secrets Act and was given £500 by MI5, which would be worth somewhere in the region of £25,000 today.

Dicketts' life as a double agent was also over although he continued to work productively for MI5 until 1943.

Chapter Nine

Second World War Executions in England

Sixteen German spies who made their way to England during the Second World War were captured and executed for their acts of espionage. Five of them, **Meier, Pons, van der Kieboom, Waldberg** and **Jakobs**, have already appeared in previous chapters of this book.

On 30 September 1940 three more German spies landed in England and were quickly arrested. **Karl Theo Drücke, Werner Heinrich Walti** and **Vera Erikson**. It was supposed to have been four but on 2 September 1940, the night before leaving for their mission, the four agents had a night of eating and drinking. On their way home their car, driven by Hilmar Dierks crashed, killing him and slightly injuring the other three. Drücke became François de Deeker, a French refugee from Belgium. When he was eventually arrested, he gave his surname to the British as Drücke. Robert Petter became Werner Heinrich Walti, and Vera stayed as Vera Erikson.

By the time the three surviving spies had fully recovered from their injuries and were fit enough to commence their mission it was 26 September, when an attempt was made by sea plane to drop them off the east coast of Scotland. But as the coastline was covered in mist and rain clouds, it was called off and the aircraft returned them to its base in Norway. By the early hours of 30 September 1940 the weather had improved sufficiently for the operation to go ahead and the three German agents were dropped off a short way out to sea off the coast of Buckie. The bicycles that they were intended to use were lost when they got out of the sea plane and were getting into their dingy and their loss meant that they had to change their plans when they reached shore.

They decided to split up, with Petter heading eastwards on his own, whilst Drücke and Vera decided to head west, which meant catching a train. They arrived at the station just before 7.30am carrying a large suitcase and costly mistake number one wasn't long in coming. Vera, obviously without thinking of the consequences, and certainly not considering that she was now in Britain, where the concerns about a German invasion were very real, asked the station master and porter for the name of the station. Winston Churchill himself had encouraged the British public to be on the lookout for German spies, so when a couple arrived at a train station that they didn't know the name of, one of them had an accent that wasn't from any part of Great Britain, and no one had ever seen them before, suspicions were quickly raised. To make matters worse when Drucke went to pay for the train he opened his wallet and it was crammed full of banknotes.

The station master then noticed that the bottom of Drucke's trousers were wet and that Erikson's shoes were also noticeably damp. This was more than enough suspicion for the station master who managed to phone the local constable without the pair knowing. Ten minutes later Constable Grieve arrived at Portgordon railway station and asked Drucke and Erikson for their identity cards, which they readily produced. Constable Grieve noticed that neither of them had an immigration stamp which they should have had on them. Not happy with the situation he asked them to accompany him to the police station, which they did. Neither of them had been searched at this stage. Once at the station Constable Grieve telephoned his Inspector who was at Buckie Police station, just over two miles away.

The Inspector arrived at Portgordon Police station a short time later, to quickly discover that the man, Drucke, could not in fact speak English and, when the Inspector began to search him, he discovered a number of rounds of ammunition on his person. Confident that they were dealing with two enemy agents the two police officers drove the pair to Buckie police station and carried out a thorough search of both of them and their property, discovering more than £400 in cash and coins, a 6.35mm Mauser automatic pistol loaded with six rounds of ammunition, a flick knife and a wireless transmitter.

Meanwhile, on leaving Drucke and Erikson, Robert Petter had walked to Buckpool railway station, only to discover that he had just missed a train to Aberdeen. He was told by the staff at the ticket office that the next train to

Aberdeen would be leaving from the neighbouring station of Buckie, just over a mile away. He made his way there where he caught the next train to Aberdeen. From there he caught another train to Edinburgh where he arrived at 4.30pm, only to discover that the next train to London wasn't due to leave until 10pm. He left his suitcase in the 'left luggage' office and went into the city to get something to eat.

What Petter didn't know was that his fellow spies, Drucke and Erikson, had already been detained and that the hunt was now on for him. News of the two detained spies and a third that was believed to still be at large, was circulated to all police stations throughout Scotland, who as part of their enquiries into locating the spy who was still at large, sent officers to all railway stations to talk to staff and check the left luggage offices. It was whilst making these enquiries at Edinburgh's Waverley station that police discovered a suitcase had recently been left there by a man who had purchased a single ticket to London. On opening the case they discovered a wireless transmitter set and knew they had found the man they were looking for. It was now a case of wait and see and hope that the man hadn't been spooked and would return to claim his suitcase, and when he did, they would arrest him.

At just after 9pm Petter returned to the station but became cautious as he got close to the left luggage office. What he didn't know was some of those purporting to be station staff were in fact police officers. He eventually entered the office, handed in his ticket and reclaimed his suitcase, and it was then that the police pounced and after a struggle removed a Mauser 6.35mm pistol that he was holding; soon afterwards a flick knife was recovered from him as well.

Petter had nearly £200 in cash on him along with documents in the name of Werner Walti, which included a British registration card and a Swiss passport. He was eventually handed over to MI5 and interrogated by Lieutenant Colonel Hinchley-Cooke.

Both Drucke and Petter went to trial at the Central Criminal Court at the Old Bailey in the City of London. The trial, which was held 'in camera' lasted for two days, 12 and 13 June 1941. They were found guilty as charged and sentenced to death. An appeal for clemency was turned down and the two men were executed by hanging at Wandsworth Prison on 6 August 1941; the sentence was carried out by Thomas Pierrepoint.

The real mystery of all of this, is what happened to Vera Erikson. She was never put on trial for any crime and never offered the opportunity to become part of the Double-Cross scheme.

MI5 files were declassified in 1999 and sent for safe keeping to the National Archives. Part of the information that has been recorded about Vera is that she had at least eight different names, six of these were recorded on passports, three of which are shown as being illegal and the other three as legal. The three legal passports are in the names of Vera Ignatieff, which was a Nansen passport. Such a passport was a certificate issued by the Nansen International Office for Refugees as an international substitute for a passport, which allowed stateless persons, or those deprived of their national passports, to enter and leave other countries. These passports were issued between 1922 and 1938. There was one in the name of Vera de Schalbourg, which was Danish and another in the name of Vera von Wedel, which was German.

The three legal passports are in the names of Vera Staritsky, Vera de Cottani, which was either Australian or Hungarian, and Vera Erikson, which was a Danish passport that had been provided by the German Intelligence Service. The seventh name comes by way of an Emergency Ration Card dated 28 February 1942, and is in the name of Veronica Edwards, Flat 904, Chelsea Cloisters, Sloane Avenue, London SW7. This is some six months after Drucke and Petter were hanged. This document alone is a strong indicator that Vera was working for MI5 in some capacity, but it also leaves the unanswered question of whether she was working for them at the time she arrived in Scotland with Drucke and Petter.

The eighth name was Vera de Cottani de Chalburg, which is the name she wrote down on a piece of paper, when asked to do so by Inspector Simpson at Buckie Police station on the day of her arrest. One of the three legal passports was in the name of Vera de Cottani.

The theories about what happened to Vera vary greatly. One account has her dying in Hamburg in 1946, whilst another claims she died in Lancashire in 1978, and yet another that after the war she was living on the Isle of Wight under an assumed name.

There is an article on Wikipedia about a Vera von Schalburg, it is definitely the same person as mentioned in this chapter but it doesn't solve any of the confusion surrounding 'Vera', it simply adds to it.

Vera von Schalburg (23 November 1907 - 1993) was a Soviet, German and British agent and sister of Christian Frederick von Schalburg.

Vera von Schalburg was born in Siberia, Russia as the second of three children to August Theodor Schalburg and wife Helene Schalburg. Her father was born 1879 in Nyborg and her mother was born 1882 in the Ukraine (possibly Poltava). She lived in Russia until the October of 1917 when she fled with her family to Denmark.

In 1920 the young von Schalburg moved with her family from Hellerup to Vibevej 14, Copenhagen, and in 1922 the family moved to Borups Alle 4, where in 1925 she still lived with her parents and youngest brother August. In Denmark she was known to the authorities as Vera Schalburg.

Later she lived in Paris where she made a living as a dancer and was a Soviet agent. There she was recruited by the Abwehr and sent to England in 1938. Her older brother C F. Von Schalburg was not pleased and believed that it would hurt his reputation and that of his party DNSAP if it became known that she had been both in German and Soviet service. In May 1939 he therefore brought up the issue with Renthe-Fink, who arranged for Vera's recall from London. She continued as an agent for Abwehr in Copenhagen until the night of 30 September 1940, where she was sent from Stavanger first by seaplane and then rubber raft to the Scottish coast near Buckie. She was joined by the two fellow agents Karl Theodore Drücke and Werner Walti.

Vera was to return to London as hostess in a fashionable tea salon in Mayfair where key politicians went. However, the three agents were quickly arrested and Drücke and Walti were convicted of espionage and hanged at Wandsworth Prison.

Vera von Schalburg survived by becoming an agent for the British. She was first taught by Klop Ustinov of MI5 and then sent to the Isle of Wight to spy on prisoners taken by Britain, while herself pretending to be a prisoner. After the war she travelled to Germany, but returned to England where she spent the rest of her life.

Although just because a particular topic has a Wikipedia page it doesn't mean that it is accurate, but this entry certainly adds a new dimension to the subject.

Karel Richard Richter was born on 29 January 1912 in Kraslice, Czechoslovakia. In his late teenage years he applied to join the Czechoslovakian Army on three occasions but was rejected each time on medical grounds. By 1935 Richter had decided a life on the ocean waves was what he wanted, so he made his way to Hamburg and managed to find employment as a machinist in the engine room of the merchant ship *Cassel* which sailed between Hamburg and Java. It would be a year before the *Cassel* returned to Hamburg. Richter then spent the next three years sailing on a number of ships backwards and forward to New York, each round trip taking twenty-seven days. With the outbreak of war his work as a machinist in the merchant navy came to an end and he returned to his home in Kraslice.

In November 1939 Richter was arrested in Sweden having been found to be in possession of false documents, and imprisoned at the Langmora Internment Camp which was one of fourteen such camps that held some 3,000 prisoners. After being held there for some eight months he was deported to Sassintz in north-east Germany. From there he was incarcerated in the Fuhlsbüttel Concentration Camp near Hamburg.

He was recruited as a spy by the *Abwehr* in November 1940, possibly whilst he was being held at Fuhlsbüttel, and undertook his training in Hamburg and the Hague in Holland. When he parachuted into England, landing near London Colney, in the early hours of 12 May 1941, he had a very specific mission, to locate another German agent by the name of Wulf

Schmidt, whose *Abwehr* code word was 'Leonhard'. The *Abwehr* were concerned about Schmidt, because they believed he had been turned by the British into working for them. Their doubts were well founded because agent Leonhard was now in fact double agent 'Tate'.

After he had landed Richter dug a hole with a small shovel and hid his parachute and equipment, but his nerves had got the better of him, possibly because the enormity and the danger of his situation had suddenly dawned on him. He hid up in the woods for a couple of days, just to gather his thoughts and calm himself before he began his journey on foot westwards along the A405 towards London, just after 10pm. He had with him a wireless set, £500 in English bank notes and $1000 American dollars, a compass, a map of East Anglia, and an automatic pistol. He was wearing an overcoat, underneath which he had on a suit, shirt and tie.

After he had only been walking for a short while, he was stopped by a lorry driver who asked him for directions to London, as all of the street signs had been removed as part of the potential invasion precautions. He was unable to provide any assistance and walked on. A short while later the lorry driver came across a police constable and repeated his question, commenting on the fact that he had just stopped a strange and unhelpful 'character' further along the road. After bidding the lorry driver goodbye, the constable peddled off down the road in the general direction the lorry driver had given him. A short while later he saw a man standing in a phone box. He asked him for his identity card which he produced, and which appeared to be in order. A condition on war time Alien identity cards was that the holder of it had to be indoors at the address on the card by 11pm each evening. The address on the card was in London and the time was already 10.30pm, causing the constable to doubt very much that the man would likely make it there in time.

The constable then asked Richter a few routine questions, one of which was where had he just come from? It was clear from one of the answers that geography wasn't one of his strong points. The answer to the question, 'Where have you just come from?' elicited the response that he had walked from the coast which had taken him a couple of hours. The constable immediately knew Richter was lying, because regardless of what direction he had come from, the nearest stretch of coastline would have taken him at least 24 hours to have walked from. The constable contacted his sergeant, who arrived a short while later in the station motor vehicle along with another constable, and together they took Richter back to their police station at Tess Road. On arrival he was questioned further and his documents examined thoroughly. His identity document said that his name was Fred Snyder, but this didn't match the details that were recorded in the expired Czechoslovakian document which was in the name of Karel Richard Richter, his actual name. The next morning, he was transferred to Hatfield Police headquarters and from there to Cannon Row Police station in London, and from there he was sent to Camp 020 at Latchmere House in West London, where he was interviewed by officers from MI5. He only changed his story when MI5 confronted him with fellow spy, Josef Jakobs. He then admitted he was a German spy and that the purpose of his mission was to locate his colleague.

His trial began at the Central Criminal Court at the Old Bailey on 21 October 1941 and lasted four days. He was charged with acts of espionage under the Treachery Act 1940. On 24 October he was found guilty as charged and sentenced to death, a decision which he appealed to the Court of Criminal Appeal. After some discussion, which included consultations with the Security Services, his appeal proved fruitless and he was hanged at Wandsworth Prison on 10 December 1941. The day didn't start off quite as might have been expected. As was normal procedure, the executioner, who on this occasion was Albert Pierrepoint, entered the condemned man's cell to tie his wrists behind his back. As Pierrepoint entered Richter's cell, he stood up and ran at the far wall head first. He fell to the cell floor, stunned. As he slowly raised himself, two prison guards jumped on him in an effort to restrain him, but he managed to fight them off and break free, before two more ran into the cell and joined in the efforts to restrain him.

Richter was eventually overpowered and Pierrepoint managed to tie his wrists behind his back with a thick leather strap. Richter was obviously an extremely strong individual as he managed to rip his hands from the bindings, something that Albert Pierrepoint had never previously seen a man do, nor did he think such a feat was possible to achieve. He certainly wasn't going to the gallows quietly or without a fight. It eventually took four warders to overpower him, so that Pierrepoint could re-apply the leather strap, before he was then forcibly manhandled to the gallows chamber. There his ankles were bound, a hood placed over his head and the noose was placed around his neck, but still he struggled. Just as Pierrepoint went to pull lever that opened the trapdoor, Richter jumped causing the noose to ride half way up his face, almost coming right off of his head, but it caught under his nose snapping his neck in the process, killing him instantly. Richter was buried in the prison garden graveyard.

In light of the struggle Richter put up immediately before he was hanged, the Constable, Alec Scott, who stopped and detained Richter on the A405, and who was one of those who conveyed him back to Tess Road Police station, appears to have been a lucky man and must have been thankful that Richter didn't put a similar struggle when he first stopped him.

Jose Estelle Key was a Gibraltarian born on 1 July 1908. He was arrested on 4 March 1942 in Gibraltar under the Emergency Powers (Defence Act) 1939, when he was found in possession of information that would be useful to an enemy, and which by all accounts he was ready to transmit to his German handlers. Sent to England, he was held at Wandsworth Prison to await his trial which was eventually held over a period of four days between 15 and 18 May 1942 at the Old Bailey in the City of London. He was charged under the Treachery Act, found guilty and sentenced to death, a verdict which he appealed. His appeal was heard and dismissed by two judges, and he was executed by hanging at Wandsworth Prison on 7 July 1942.

Alphonse Louis Eugene Timmerman was born in Ostend, Belgium on 1 August 1904. When Germany occupied Belgium on 20 May 1940, Timmerman decided to make his way to England and join the Free Belgian Merchant Navy. His route of choice was to travel through Spain, but when he reached the French/Spanish border, he was arrested and imprisoned in Barcelona. After months of political efforts by the Belgian Consul in Barcelona, he was released and allowed to travel to Lisbon in Portugal, where his name was added to the list of Belgian refugees who were waiting to make their way to England.

Timmerman finally found passage on a ship bound for England at the end of August 1941, arrived in London on 1 September and was immediately arrested for having false identity papers. Initially he was sent to the Royal Victoria Patriotic School, which was also known as the London Reception Centre. During the Second World War, some 30,000 refugees were interviewed or interrogated there.

Timmerman was interviewed by a Belgian Security officer. Such interviews also included a thorough search of any cases, bags or other belongings that an interviewee had with them. In Timmerman's belongings, his interviewer discovered an envelope which contained white powder, a bunch of orange sticks and a piece of cotton wool. To the uninitiated there would be nothing too suspicious about those items, but to the trained eyes of those working at the London Reception Centre, these were all items used in sending secret letters. Timmerman was questioned further about these items and was asked what they were and how they came to be in his possession. His response was that he had been given them by a Spanish Communist whilst he was in prison in Barcelona. His story was not accepted and he was charged under the Treachery Act,

At both the London Reception Centre and Camp 020, which was situated in West London, Timmerman confessed to his interviewers that he had come to Britain to obtain Allied naval and aircraft information. He appeared in court at the Old Bailey on 20 May 1942 where he was found guilty and sentenced to death. His appeal was heard on the same day as Key's and dismissed. He was hanged alongside Key at Wandsworth Prison on 7 July 1942.

Johannes Marinus Dronkers was born on the outskirts of Amsterdam, Holland on 3 April 1896. In the early morning of 18 May 1942, he was picked up whilst in a small boat in the North Sea along with two other Dutchmen. The three men were definitely not refugees who were escaping the Nazi rule and occupation of their country, but agents who worked for the German *Abwehr*, whose mission was to inform their German spy masters of Britain's state of war readiness and preparation. The obvious question in Dronkers case was why wasn't he offered the opportunity by MI5, as many other *Abwehr* agents had been, to become part of their Double-Cross system?

Franciscus Johannes Winter was born in Antwerp, Belgium, on 17 January 1903. In the early months of 1942 he arrived in Spain stating that he was a Belgian refugee, having escaped from Nazi tyranny, and wanted to get to England. His wish was duly granted and he arrived in the UK on board a British registered ship on 31 July 1942. On arrival he was interviewed as to who he was and what was he intending to do now that he was in England.

The story he gave to British authorities was that he had escaped from his native Belgium after Germany had invaded. He then made his way across France, which by then was also occupied by German forces, and arrived in Spain where he was arrested and imprisoned. When he was subsequently released, having adequately answered all of the questions asked of him, he offered his services to the British authorities, in whichever way he could assist the Allied war effort. His approach, it has to be said, was unusual, which in part made those interviewing him, suspicious of his real intentions. Found in his possession was a total of about £100 in British, French, American, Belgian and Spanish currencies. This only made the interviewing officers even more suspicions of who Winter was, and what his true intentions were.

Not surprisingly, his story was not believed, and he was re-interviewed by British Counter Intelligence officers. He repeated his desire to be of service to the Allies, adding that he would like to join the Free Belgian forces or obtain employment on board a Belgian ship. Winter was told by his interrogators that they simply did not believe his story, but he persisted and again they told him that they didn't believe what he was telling them. Then remarkably, and obviously clueless as to the full ramifications of what he was about to say, he totally changed his story and admitted that what he had said was a pack of lies. He then made a statement, one that it can only be assumed he did not appreciate, and which was, in essence, the signing of his own death warrant. He admitted that he was working for the *Abwehr* and had been sent by them to report on the movement of convoys in which he sailed. He explained in great detail how he had been given training in the preparation and use of secret ink and an address in a neutral country, where he could safely send his reports.

His trial took place at the Old Bailey on 4 December 1942, where he was charged under the Treachery Act, found guilty and sentenced to death. He appealed the decision, but it was dismissed by two Crown Court Judges on 11 January 1943, and he was hanged at Wandsworth Prison on 26 January 1943, executed by Albert Pierrepoint and Henry Critchell.

Oswald John Job was born in Stepney, London on 4 July 1885, but his parents were both German. He had moved to live in France when he was 26 years old in 1911. When Germany invaded and occupied France in 1940, Job was interned as he held a British passport. Whilst in detention in Paris he became friendly with his German guards, who passed this information to their superiors. At the same time SS General Günther Sachs had been instructed by Himmler to look at new ways of sending spies to Britain, as he was unhappy with the failings of Admiral Canaris when it came to the spying game. He was approached by an SS officer and agreed to work for Nazi Germany as one of their agents and was immediately taken to Spain. He was instructed to go to the British Embassy in Madrid where he told them he had escaped from an internment camp in Paris and had made contact with the French Underground. His story was made more believable due to the state of his physical appearance which, having spent some months in different French prisons, had left him looking emaciated.

It was members of the German Secret Service who had conveyed him to the French/Spanish border. There he was handed over to Spanish Falangists working with the Germans who took him to Madrid. At the British Embassy, his situation was helped greatly when one of the officials recognised him as they had gone to the same public school. After that stroke of good fortune his story was believed without question, and a British Embassy official personally conveyed him to Lisbon, where he was put on an aircraft and flown to England.

He was further vetted without any concerns or questions, released and provided with a National Assistance Board allowance, which allowed him to rent a room in a property in Bayswater, London. His instructions from his spy masters in Germany were to report on bomb damage caused by Luftwaffe air raids and any visible preparations for an invasion by German forces. The letters, on the surface, appeared to be quite innocent, their content being on routine day to day matters such as the weather, how they were keeping, and their hopes for the future. But in between the lines of writing was further information of a more sinister nature, written in secret ink.

Soon after arriving in England, the British Postal Censorship Service noticed an unusually high number of letters being sent by members of Job's family to his former friends and fellow inmates at the St Denis internment camp in Paris. As it was such a marked number, and the bulk of the letters were purportedly being sent by members of Job's family rather than himself, the Postal Censorship Service passed this information on to the British Secret Service, who decided to contact Job's relatives who had supposedly sent the letters. When interviewed all of Job's relatives denied having ever sent letters. With this information to hand, the British security services asked members of the Metropolitan Police Special Branch, to pay Job a visit at his address in Bayswater, which they did on 1 November 1943. They searched his room, despite his annoyance, and much to their surprise they found nothing. Unfortunately for Job one of the detectives noticed something slightly at odds and not in keeping with the situation. Job only had one room and had arrived in England with no luggage, yet he had a fob with a large number of keys on it. Job and his unusually large set of keys were taken to Scotland Yard, where he was interviewed and the keys were examined more closely. The bunch of five keys were discovered to be hollow, each containing a chemical for use in 'invisible writing'. The tips of the keys were specially designed so that they could be used as a 'pen'.

His trial took place at the Old Bailey between 24 and 26 January 1944, where he was charged with offences under the Treachery Act. His defence was that he had agreed to become a spy for the Germans, purely as a means of getting to England, and that he had never had any intention of carrying out any spying activities for the Germans. Despite this claim he could not explain why he hadn't handed himself in on his arrival in England, or why he had subsequently sent letters to his German spy masters. He was found guilty, sentenced to death, and executed by hanging at Pentonville Prison on 16 March 1944.

Pierre Richard Charles Neukermans was born in Waarbecke, Belgium on 1 May 1916, a child of the First World War. As a young man, he became a soldier in the Belgian Army, but after being injured he was invalided out in 1938.

After the invasion of Belgium in May 1940 and the subsequent occupation of his country by German forces, Neukermans tried to escape, but his attempts proved fruitless and he returned to his life in Brussels. The when, why or how he was recruited by the *Abwehr*, is unknown, but he was approached by them and agreed to become one of their agents. After his training in sabotage, wireless transmissions and the writing of secret messages, he was taken to neutral Portugal, and then arrived in England on a flight from Lisbon, having convinced the British authorities that he was a loyal Belgian subject who had escaped the Nazi occupation of his country and wanted to help the Allied war effort. Neukermans was not the first Belgian to make such claims having travelled a similar route and wanting to help the Allied war effort. He further explained that he made a previous attempt at escape from Belgium, when he had been helped by two men whom he only knew as 'Louis' and 'Georges', who had managed to get him as far as Paris. It seemed a strange thing to highlight, as it wasn't something he had been questioned about, he had simply offered up the story. Sometimes, too much information can be just as suspicious as too little.

He arrived in England on 16 July 1943 and partly because of his previous experience as an officer in the Belgian Army, he acquired a job as a clerk in the Belgian government in exile that was situated in London. The bulk of the Belgian government was in premises at Eaton Square, in the Belgravia area of West London, which before the war had been the location of the Belgian Embassy. Other departments of the Belgian government were in nearby Hobart Place, Belgrave Square and Knightsbridge.

On 2 February 1944, Neukermans was arrested by the British Secret Service after being discovered sending information of Allied convoy movements between Britain and the Belgian Congo, to Louis Debray and Georges Hollevoet in Brussels. These two individuals were the same 'Louis and Georges' who helped Neukerman get to Paris. Both men actually worked for the SS and were Neukermans' spy masters.

When questioned about his actions, he admitted that he was in fact a German agent, and that after having arrived in England, he wrote letters containing secret writing to an address in a neutral country. This address had been given to him by the German Secret Service, prior to his departure from Lisbon. The content of the letters, which had been written in invisible ink, also included detailed information about where Belgian troops were stationed in the UK.

His trial saw him facing charges under the Treachery Act for which there was only one possible sentence – death. It lasted for four days between 28 April and 1 May 1944, and he was found guilty. He appealed his sentence which was dismissed, the case being held on 8 June 1944. He was hanged by Albert Pierrepoint and Alex Riley on Friday 23 June 1944, at Pentonville Prison.

An interesting footnote to Neukermans' case was that the day after he was hanged, the Home Office made an announcement in the Press concerning his execution. They noticeably provided much more detailed information than was usual, especially in relation to enemy agents. An argument could be made that the reason for such a report naming the executed agent as well as his two handlers, was simply to let the German intelligence services know that they knew the names and location of their two spy handlers.

Joseph Jan Vanhove owns what is quite possibly one of the most unwanted moments in the history of the Second World War as he was the last German agent to be executed. A soldier killed on the battlefield, a pilot killed during a dogfight, or a sailor perishing in one of the oceans of the world, could be said to have died with honour; being executed as a spy does not.

When Germany invaded Belgium in May 1940, Vanhove was working as a waiter in Antwerp, as well as supplementing his meagre wages by dabbling in the black market. Without any warning, in June 1942, he offered to work for the German Intelligence Service, who readily accepted his offer. His first job as an agent of the *Abwehr* saw him sent to France to spy on French and Belgian workers and the airfields they were helping to build for the Germans in northern France. His main purpose was to discover which, if any, of the workers were involved, or believed to be involved, in resistance-related activities.

The *Abwehr* later attempted to get Vanhove to England via Switzerland, but the plan failed and he had no option but to return to Belgium. Not to be put off, the Germans later sent him to Stockholm in neutral Sweden where he visited the British Embassy and offered to fight for the Allies. It seemed strange as on the whole Sweden remained neutral throughout the Second World War, although at different times during that period she directly or indirectly provided help to both sides.

The Embassy staff immediately suspected him of being a German spy but allowed him to catch a ship to England. There was, however, method to their madness, because as soon as the ship arrived on 11 February 1943, and much to his surprise, he was arrested. He was then interviewed about who he was and what his real intentions were for wanting to come to the UK. He eventually admitted that he was an enemy spy and had come to the UK to carry out work as a German agent.

He was charged under the Treachery Act and his trial took place before Mr Justice Hallett at the Old Bailey over 23 and 24 May 1944. After all the evidence had been heard, he was found guilty as charged and sentenced to death. As was normal in such cases, an appeal was made on behalf of Vanhove, more out of hope than expectation, but that was dismissed on 27 June, and he was hanged at Pentonville Prison on Wednesday, 12 July 1944.

Theodore William John Schurch, the son of a Swiss father and English mother, was born in Hammersmith, London on 5 May 1918, and was hanged at Pentoville Prison on 4 January 1946. He enlisted in the British Army in 1936 just after he turned 18 and was posted to the Royal Army Service Corps as a driver.

Schurch was captured at the Battle of Gazala, near Tobruk, Libya, in North Africa. The battle was a resounding victory for the Axis powers and not long after his capture he agreed to work for both the Italian and German intelligence services and was placed in different prisoner of war camps to try and illicit information from unsuspecting Allied prisoners. He was arrested in Rome in March 1945 and was returned to England and charged with nine counts of treachery along with desertion with intent to join the enemy. His court martial took place during September 1945, at the Duke of York's Headquarters in Chelsea. Overseeing the proceedings was Major Melford Stevenson, who also served in the same position during war crimes trials in Hamburg at the end of the Second World War.

Schurch, who was 27 years of age, was found guilty as charged and sentenced to death. He was hanged by Albert Pierrepoint on 4 January 1946 at Pentonville Prison, which also made him the last person to be executed in England for an offence other than murder, as well as being the only British soldier executed for treason during the Second World War.

The following group of individuals were not spies who were sent to the UK by Germany, but were British subjects who willingly worked for and took sides with the Nazis, against their country of birth. Some of them were subsequently sentenced to death and hanged in British prisons and their stories should also be included.

Duncan Alexander Croall Scott-Ford was born in Plymouth, Devon on 4 September 1921, and went on to become a seaman in the British Merchant Navy. He was executed on 3 November 1942, under the Treachery Act, for supplying relevant information to the enemy during a time of war.

Initially he had served in the Royal Navy, enlisting when he was just 16 years of age. His first posting was HMS *Impregnable*, a shore establishment at Devonport. In 1939, just two months away from the outbreak of the Second World War, he was serving on board HMS *Gloucester* when it docked at Dar-es-Salaam in Tanzania. Whilst in port he met, and quickly became infatuated with a pretty young German girl. Although there was no actual evidence to prove it, the British Security Services had a strong belief that he had passed her secret naval codes, which if true would strongly suggest she was working for the German intelligence services.

In 1940 he was stationed in Egypt and this time his attention was drawn to a local prostitute who worked nearby, and who he saw on a regular basis. To pay for this he made alterations to his post office savings book to make it look like there was more money in the account. This came to the attention of the naval authorities, and after they had carried out their own investigation, it was decided to put him before a court martial where he was found guilty, sentenced to two years imprisonment and dismissed from the service. Fortunately for Scott-Ford, his mother was a stoic individual, who decided that the sentence her son had been given was too severe. She then appealed the decision successfully which resulted in her son's sentence being reduced to just six months and his naval record being endorsed with the words, 'honourable discharge'.

Scott-Ford served his sentence in England and was released in July 1941 and shortly afterwards he enlisted in the Merchant Navy. On 10 May 1942 the ship he was serving on, the SS *Finland*, arrived in Lisbon, Portugal. Whilst enjoying some shore leave Scott-Ford was on his own drinking in one of the city's many bars, when he was approached by a man he didn't know. They got into a conversation and the man said that his name was Rithman. This was no chance meeting even if Scott-Ford didn't immediately realise it. Rithman made sure that he had his attention by telling him that he could get a letter to the girl he had known in Dar-es-Salaam. It can only be guessed at as to what Scott-Ford's initial reaction was, but whatever it was Rithman wasn't put off. He wanted to know whether all British ships had been ordered to be in port by 28 June. It wasn't a question he knew the answer to but he told Rithman that he would try and find out and the two men agreed to meet the following day. Scott-Ford was unable to find the answer to Rithman's question, but they still met up. This time there was a third man present who introduced himself as Captain Henley, he wasted no time in bombarding Scott-Ford with a number of questions including what was the morale of the British public like, what did they think about Winston Churchill and what was the true extent of damage caused by

German air raids. At the end of the meeting Scott-Ford was given a 1,000 escudo note for the information he provided.

Before his ship sailed he met the two men again when they asked him even more questions including the location of British minefields along the southern coast of England, and how many and how often American servicemen were arriving in Britain.

When the SS *Finland* arrived back at Liverpool, all of the crew including Scott-Ford were asked if any of them had been approached by anybody who could have been, or they knew to have been a German agent. Scott-Ford said he believed that he had been, but didn't say anything, which was of course a lie. Whether he realised it or not, and regardless of what his intentions were, he had made a mistake which was traceable back to him. When Captain Henley had given him the 1,000 escudo note, he had asked him to sign a receipt for it, which he did.

The SS *Finland*, with Scott-Ford as one of its crew, returned to Lisbon on 26 July 1942, where he once again met up with Richman and Captain Henley. This time the meeting had a different feel to it. Henley and Richman were more pushy, demanding and threatening, but gave Scott-Ford another 500 escudos, which they once again asked him to sign for, which he did. They then threatened to hand over the two receipts he had signed for the escudos to the British Embassy. Maybe because he had suddenly realised the vulnerable position he was in, he provided Henley and Richman with information about the convoy the SS *Finland* was a part of, the location of an aircraft factory in southern England and Allied troops training for an invasion of Europe.

The SS *Finland* arrived back in England on 18 August 1942, this time at Salford Docks in Manchester. As was the normal routine, Scott-Ford was questioned as to whether he had been approached by anybody whilst in Lisbon. On this occasion, he not only admitted that he had been approached, but also that he had been paid a total of 1,600 escudos for some information which he had provided. The British authorities had intelligence that the Germans had one of their spies, who went by the code name of Rutherford, operating in Lisbon.

Scott-Ford was arrested and sent to the London Reception Centre where refugees arriving in England were sent and questioned in detail to try an uncover any German agents who were trying to slip into the country unannounced. His quarters on board the SS *Finland* were searched and notes he had made about the convoy he had been part of, were discovered.

Scott-Ford was detained under Defence Regulation 18B which allowed people who were suspected of being Nazi sympathisers to be detained without trial, and also suspended an individual's right to *habeas corpus*. He was sent to Camp 020 at Latchmere House in south west London where he was interrogated by officials from MI5, with whom he was both open and co-operative, although as time went on Scott-Ford began to realise the precarious situation he was now in. When he was unable to offer any more than the information he had already come up with, he was charged under the Treachery Act. It might have been that those interviewing him believed he was not being truthful, but they certainly did not consider him to be useful enough for the Double-Cross scheme.

Scott-Ford's day in court came on 16 October 1942. It was held in secret before Mr Justice Birkett, who was one of the Judges at the Nuremberg trials. He was found guilty of the charges against him, and the only sentence allowed under the Act was death. Those in charge at Camp 020 were asked for their views on whether they felt Scott-Ford should be reprieved. Despite his openness and frankness with them whilst being interrogated, the reply was that as far as they were concerned they could think of no reason why his death sentence should be amended, and went as far as saying:

> Indeed, there may well be many who will agree that death by hanging is almost too good for a sailor who will encompass the death of thousands of his shipmates without qualm.

At 9am on 3 November 1942, Albert Pierrepoint carried out the execution of Scott-Ford by hanging at Wandsworth Prison.

An interesting article appeared in the *Reading Evening Post* newspaper dated Tuesday 11 February 1986.

Traitor Hanged

A sharply contrasting picture of how Britain dealt with wartime traitors has been disclosed in newly released Home Office files. Merchant seaman Duncan Scott-Ford, aged 21, was hanged in Wandsworth Jail in 1942 for selling convoy secrets to the Germans. But Ralph Powell, nephew of Scouting movement founder Lord Baden Powell, received only a warning after he admitted broadcasting Nazi propaganda for three years.

John Amery was a pro-Nazi British fascist who, during the Second World War, was the person who proposed to the Wehrmacht the formation of what would be called the British Volunteer Force, which later in the war would become the British Free Corps. He also helped making recruitment efforts and propaganda broadcasts for Nazi Germany. He came from a very well-to-do family. His father John Amery was a Conservative Member of Parliament and government minister. What made his actions even more distasteful was the fact that Amery's mother was a Hungarian Jew who had converted to Protestantism.

He married Una Wing, a former prostitute, when he was 21 years of age. The fact that Amery was a staunch anti-communist may be the real reason why he so readily came to embrace the Nazi version of National Socialism, because he saw it as the only real alternative to Russian Bolshevism. In 1936, he quit England to live in France, but he also spent some time travelling round Europe looking at the effect of fascism in different countries.

Later the same year he joined the Spanish Nationalists under Franco's leadership during the Spanish Civil War and worked as an intelligence officer with Italian volunteer forces, even winning a medal of honour for his work. After the end of the war he returned to living in France and remained there after the German invasion of the country began in June 1940. After France surrendered on 22 June 1940, Amery found himself in the area that was under the control of the Vichy French Government. He didn't want to be there, but despite his best attempts to leave, he couldn't get out, because the French authorities wouldn't let him. That was where he remained until September 1942, when Hauptmann Werner Plack managed to get Amery the required documentation to get him out of the country and into Germany. He travelled with Plack to Berlin so that he could speak with members of the German English Committee.

One of Amery's suggestions was for Nazi Germany to form a British anti-Bolshevik Legion. Word of this suggestion reached the ears of Hitler who was mightily impressed with the young Amery and allowed him to stay in Germany as a guest of the Reich. Amery was more than happy to make a number of pro-German propaganda radio broadcasts in an effort to get Britain's to fight against the perceived threat of communism.

Amery had not forgotten his idea of forming a British unit to fight for the Nazis, recruiting up to 100 men, who he could then use to attract even more recruits. With easy access to tens of thousands of British prisoners of war, he had a ready-made army of potential recruits just waiting to engage with him.

When he was ready Amery paid a visit to the Saint-Denis prisoner of war camp just outside Paris. He spoke to some fifty British and Commonwealth prisoners about his plans of forming a unit of British and Allied troops to fight alongside the Germans in their battle against the Russians and the threat from communism. Despite handing out leaflets outlining what he was trying to achieve, there was not an ounce of interest amongst those he was talking to. But he wasn't deterred by his failure and on another occasion he actually managed to interest two prisoners of war to enlist in his madcap scheme.

Kenneth Edward Jordan Berry and **Alfred Minchin** ended up joining the British Free Corps and wore German uniforms with a small Union Jack on the lower part of the left sleeve.

As for Amery, he continued to carry out radio broadcasts for the Nazis out of Berlin until the latter part of 1944, when he was sent to Northern Italy as support for Benito Mussolini's Salò Republic, although it is debateable as to just how helpful he could have been. Amery was arrested, along with his French girlfriend, Michelle Thomas, by Italian partisans near Como on 25 April 1945. From there they were sent to Milan where they were handed over to British authorities. The intelligence officer who arrested Amery was a British officer by the name of Alan Whicker, who after the war in 1957 joined the BBC, and in 1958 began his travel programme entitled '*Whickers' World*' which continued well in to the 1990s.

Amery's trial for treason began at the Old Bailey on 28 November 1945, which became an interesting affair, full of twists and turns. At a preliminary hearing his brother John claimed that Amery had in fact become a Spanish citizen which meant he could not legally have committed treason against the United Kingdom. Amery also argued that he was anti-communist and not a Nazi, and had never attacked nor tried to encourage others, of attacking their own country. It didn't stop there. Amery's council, Gerald Osborne Slade KC, attempted to show, and certainly claimed, that his client was mentally ill.

All attempts by Amery and his legal team to try and bring his mental state of mind into the equation, failed. But before the day was out, and with the court packed to the rafters, to everybody's shock and surprise, Amery suddenly pleaded guilty to the charges that he faced and was immediately sentenced to death; but not before the Judge, Mr Justice Humphreys, who was just as shocked as anybody else, checked that Amery fully understood the consequences of pleading guilty, and that the only sentence he could give was death by hanging. Satisfied that Amery did understand the consequences of what he was pleading guilty to, Mr Justice Humphreys read out his verdict:

> John Amery, I am satisfied that you knew what you did and that you did it intentionally and deliberately after you had received warnings from your fellow countrymen that the course you were pursuing, amounted to high treason. They called you a traitor and you heard them; but in spite of that you continued in that course. You now stand a self-confessed traitor to your King and country, and you have forfeited your right to live.

On 19 December 1945, Amery was hanged at Wandsworth Prison, and then buried in the prison's cemetery.

Of the two men who were seduced by Amery into joining the British Free Corps, Kenneth Edward Jordan Berry and Alfred Minchin, Berry was a boy seaman in the Merchant Navy who was taken prisoner of war in 1940 when the ship he was serving aboard, was sunk by the Germans. Whilst being held as a prisoner of war in France, he was persuaded by John Amery to join the British Free Corps as part of the Waffen-SS. Berry continued to serve with his unit until 29 April 1945 but could not be found when the Corps were preparing to leave Neustrelitz and they left without him. When he was returned to England after the war, he was put on trial, found guilty, but miraculously, he somehow did not receive the death penalty, but instead received only a nine-month prison sentence, the lightest sentence passed on any traitor from the Second World War.

Having run away from home at the age of 14 after being caught stealing, he enrolled in the Merchant Navy after claiming that he was a year older. He got a job as part of the crew of a British oil tanker, *Cymbeline*, that sailed from Gibraltar on 27 May 1940, en route to Trinidad. Although they were a ship of the Merchant Navy, they were sailing on behalf of the British Admiralty, which made her even more of a target. On 2 September 1940, the *Cymberline* was attacked and sunk by the German merchant vessel, the *Widder*, which had been converted into a heavily armed cruiser. Although the *Cymberline* incurred casualties, Berry was one of those who survived and who was picked up by the German vessel and held on board her for six weeks, before being taken ashore and sent to a prisoner of war camp in the far east of France at Besancon, and following that at St Denis on the outskirts of Paris. Whilst at the latter he escaped and made his way into the centre of Paris, where he became a black marketeer, selling whatever he could. He was eventually recaptured and interrogated by the Gestapo, who were desperate to discover who had helped him escape from the prisoner of war camp. He readily gave up those who had helped him and did not seem in the least perturbed at the thought of what might happen to them. The word had got out about what he had done and when he was returned to the prisoner of war camp from where he had escaped, he was shunned by the other prisoners.

After Berry had heard a talk given by Amery with the stated objective of fighting alongside the German Army on the eastern front, he decided to join the British Free Corps of which Amery had spoken. Berry, along with three other prisoners of war, were moved to accommodation at Avenue Exelmans in Paris. It would be fair to say that Berry wasn't the brightest of individuals, due largely to his lack of education. It is claimed he believed that John Amery was the British Foreign Secretary Leo Amery, who was actually John Amery's father.

After spending a few months in Paris, Berry and those with him were moved on to Berlin to continue their training, and in November 1943, he became a member of the British Free Corps, which by then was under the control of the Waffen-SS. Berry was sent to Genshagen in north-east Germany where he met up with other British Free Corps recruits, Roy Courlander, William Brittain, Frank McLardy, and Martin and Alfred Minchin.

From June 1944 all members of the British Free Corps, including Berry, began wearing SS uniforms, the only thing distinguishing them from normal SS soldiers, was the Union Jack emblem on the lower part of their left sleeve.

In June 1944, a chance incident took place involving Berry that might just have saved his life. Along with Alfred Minchin, Berry was visiting prisoner of war camps, looking to recruit new members for the British Free Corps. They were in the area of Westertimke, when Berry was recognised by a number of British Merchant Navy sailors from his old ship, the *Cymbeline*, who were on a working party. He got into conversation with a few of them who told him that no matter what the Germans had told him, Germany was losing the war, and that he should get out of his German uniform and return to becoming a prisoner of war.

Whatever it was that was said to him, made an impression. At the nearby prisoner of war camp he sought out the senior British officer, Captain Robert Finlay-Notman, and requested advice as to how he could get out of the British Free Corps. Before he left he handed a letter to Captain Finlay-Notman, officially asking for help.

Looking back on the situation through today's eyes, it appears strange how quickly and easily he went from being a staunch member of the British Free Corps, to no longer wanting to be part of them, purely based on a conversation with ex crew mates, who could after all have been lying to him. They weren't, but he wasn't to know that.

Four months later Berry's situation couldn't have become any worse. On 11 October 1944, he was moved to Dresden to undergo combat engineer training, where he was issued with a rifle and now had to carry out military duties. With the war in Europe six months from its end, Berry was assigned to the 3rd Company of the 11th SS Armoured Reconnaissance Unit on 22 March 1945, who were situated in the vicinity of the River Oder, but by the beginning of May, German forces were in full retreat. As Berry's unit prepared to leave, they could not find him anywhere. He was subsequently discovered by troops of the advancing Red Army. He had discarded his German SS uniform, and because of his accent, the Russians just assumed that he was an escaped British prisoner of war and handed him over to the first group of Americans that they came in to contact with. Assuming that he was in fact an escaped British prisoner of war, they flew him back to England on 12 May 1945, and from there he made his way home, to Penryn in Cornwall.

The New Zealander, Roy Courlander, who had also joined the British Free Corps, was captured by Allied forces in September 1944, in Belgium, and interrogated by British intelligence officers, during which Berry's name came up and he was added to the list of wanted members of the British Free Corps. Berry was interviewed by British intelligence officers on 3 July and 3 November 1945, at which time he gave a full and frank account of his wartime service, including both his time in the Merchant Navy and the British Free Corps.

On 3 September 1945, Canadian soldier Edward Bernard Martin, of the Canadian Essex Scottish Regiment, who had served with the British Free Corps, appeared before a court-martial in Farnborough, Hampshire. During his trial he named forty men whose names he knew, who had also served in the British Free Corps. One of these men was Kenneth Berry. He appeared before Bow Street Magistrates Court on

2 January 1946, after having been arrested, and held in custody since 20 December 1945. He was charged under the Defence Regulations Act, 'with other others not presently in custody and with others unknown, to do acts with intent to assist the enemy, namely, to join the British Free Corps'.

Positive comments about him by others possibly helped save his life. Two witnesses, Captain Notman, and German military adviser Wilhelm Roessler, who interrogated Berry, both spoke of his immaturity and naivety, Roessler going as far as to say he was 'a young fool who did not know what he was doing'. The Director of Public Prosecutions called Berry 'an irresponsible youth who was easily led'. Berry was found guilty and given a nine month prison sentence, the shortest ever given to anybody convicted of such an offence. Berry was in a German Army unit, in German uniform, carrying a loaded rifle and fighting alongside members of the Waffen-SS. John Amery's major crime was to carry out radio broadcasts trying to convince British and Allied prisoners of war to join the British Free Corps and fight against the Russians. His punishment was to be hanged.

Reading through some of the individual cases, it is absolutely staggering the differences in sentencing. A good example of this would be Kenneth Berry and John Amery. Even more amazing was that in 1946, Berry once again went back to sea with the Merchant Navy. Whilst neither Amery nor Berry were German spies sent to England to carry out acts of espionage for the Nazis, nevertheless the acts they committed were for and on behalf of Hitler and Nazi Germany.

George Johnson Armstrong was the first British citizen to be executed under the Treachery Act. He was hanged by Thomas Pierrepoint at Wandsworth Prison on 10 July 1941, his trial having taken place at the Old Bailey on 8 May 1941, when he was charged under Section 1 of the Treachery Act 1940 of communicating with the German Consul in Boston, America and offering his services to Nazi Germany. He had been arrested in Boston, Massachusetts, for being a spy and deported to England.

His method of contacting the Germans in Boston was by writing a letter to Dr Herbert Scholz at the Consul. It was dated 19 November 1940:

Dear Sir,

Please excuse this somewhat unusual method of address, this letter may come to you by messenger, or failing in his effort to do so, it will reach you by mail. I am an officer of the British Service, an engineer at recent date attached to the Inspection of Aircraft Department (AID) in England. Latterly I was transferred to the Marine Department under control of the British Admiralty. My intention is to make German contacts here in the US which may be beneficially used on my return to England. Naturally in the various capabilities in which I was employed in England, I have information which would be very valuable in the proper sources. You will no doubt agree with me that it is not advisable to enter into any written discussion upon this subject here at this time, but if you could have someone contact me who was reliable then the matter could be more fully gone in to.

I was detained by the US Immigration authorities before I could make any such contacts here in the US and have been transferred from East Boston Immigration Station to Deer Island to be held pending deportation proceedings. I feel that the information which I have and the value of someone so placed in England in these times would be greatly appreciated by yourself or those who you would put in contact with me.

Truly yours
George Armstrong.

PS. My mail is censored by the Immigration authorities but this letter will not pass through the official channels, a direct contact by visit would be the most advisable.

Armstrong's defence was quite an interesting one. Before the outbreak of the Second World War he had met a man in England by the name of

Dr Carl Klein. When war broke out Armstrong made his way to New York where he frequented different bars across the city. At one of them he met a German woman by the name of Alice Hahn and noticed how she used her womanly charms to get chatting with British sailors, the purpose of which was to illicit information from them when their ships were sailing between New York and the UK. During his time in New York he also met Dr Klein, who just happened to turn up at the same bar where Armstrong had met Alice Hahn. Coincidence? Maybe not.

Unrelated to his being arrested and deported back to England, Armstrong had previously been arrested in Boston and sent to Deer Island Internment Camp, where he found Dr Klein who told him that he, Alice and a few others had all been arrested, and that to try and prevent their deportation back to Germany, they were liaising with Dr Herbert Scholz from the German Consul in Boston. Whilst Klein was out of his cell, being interrogated, Armstrong looked through his paperwork and found a letter that had been sent to him by Dr Scholz in which he said he had a list of German agents who were working in the UK. That seems highly unlikely assuming Dr Scholz and Dr Klein were not well acquainted. Why would he trust a man with such delicate, and presumably secret information? Was it all part of a plan to gain Armstrong's interest?

In his defence Armstrong claimed that knowing Dr Scholz had such a list made him determined to make contact with him, and pretend that he was interested in helping Nazi Germany in their efforts in the UK, just so that he could find out the names of the spies and pass them on to the British authorities. Although a plausible story, it was not one that the jury believed, and so it was that Armstrong was found guilty and sentenced to death.

The following is a statement that Armstrong made to the British Police after he had arrived back in England having been deported from America.

My observations made at Halifax N.S Central Convoy base for British Ships crossing the Atlantic with war materials, have only served to verify the fact that this aforementioned Nazi ring is operating in conjunction with agents in the U.K and Canada.

During the time I was in the Immigration Station in Halifax, which is also being used as a hospital, a repatriation centre, and practically a dumping ground for foreign seamen all mixing together, I learned that it was common knowledge just when the convoy conferences were being attended by the various Captains of ships assembled in Bedford Basin to make up convoys. Further, it was known just what cargo each ship carried & how much, the name of the ships in the convoy, whether steam or motor ships, the speed of the convoys, the number of vessels, the Commodore ship, the armament of these ships, & what is more important, the sailing time & circle upon which the course was laid.

I was informed as to ship movements hours before some of them even arrived in Halifax. One particular instance was that the *Duchess of York* was due to arrive with troops. Two days later this ship did arrive in Bedford basin as had been stated. It is little to be wondered at that Halifax is full of survivors of torpedoes and sabotaged ships, and it is a matter which presents no difficulty whatever to plant elements of sabotage in the holds of ships which are taking cargoes in Halifax, New York, New Jersey and Boston, but more especially in Halifax where the officials are wantonly lax in their duty and speech.

Anyone at any time can procure information and access to ships in this port, and incidents such as that which led to the loss of the *Black Osprey* and others of quite recent date substantiate the fact that many of the ships torpedoed in convoy, do not occur until some vessel in the convoy has become a beacon which discloses the position & course of the convoy at night. Ships can be and are loaded at widely diversified points, and may lay in Halifax for weeks & nothing occurs; but it is common to have explosions taking place in the holds or some other accessible part of the ship when in convoy, after leaving Halifax. This is common knowledge among members of the Merchant Navy & is the subject of much discussion.

This condition can all be traced to information leaking out in Halifax while the ships are making up a convoy. Troop ships are known, the number of men and the regiment to which they belong. Few seamen are English speaking or of English descent in the Immigration Station & German is spoken by many. These men have the privilege of staying in the Station and visiting in the town of Halifax at their wish at night. Anyone without censure can telephone to anyone in the town, I have done it. Therefore, there is nothing to hinder and much to assist anyone passing information to whom they wish.

The fact remains that many lives are lost, thousands of tons of shipping and millions of dollars worth of valuable war materials simply by the gross carelessness & wanton neglect of the Officials responsible for the suppression of such conditions. My interest is and has been solely from a Merchant Navy point of view, it is with this purpose in mind at all times that I have jeopardised my own security to produce some concrete evidence that would lead me to an investigation of the officials concerned and the apprehension of the agents who use the information so procured.

Furthermore, I am convinced that if permitted to do so, that working along the lines as outlined in my previous statement with those executive agents, I should be able to procure the complete list of the agents residing & operating in England.

There is little or no check upon persons going aboard ships in Halifax while loading. Stevedores and others who are presumed to be officials, but whom no one questions, are permitted to wander at their leisure about the ships until the vessel is in the stream again at which time naval ratings check passes, but only sometimes.

Although I was not myself aware of the fact, an acquaintance of mine called me by telephone and wished me goodbye, told me I was sailing the following day at 3pm without convoy and such did turn out to be the case; and this particular person has no interest in shipping whatever; it is just another example of information being bandied about by careless officials who are entrusted with this responsibility.

It is my sincere hope that responsible officials in England will be interested in repairing this condition & thereby giving such members of the British Merchant Navy who are willing & anxious to bring these ships & cargoes to England at least a fifty-fifty chance of survival; at all events closing off this source of information & sabotage.

If there is not some ulterior motive in it, why are passengers permitted after being on ships permitted to change their mind & leave the ships in Halifax, some of them having spent more than a week aboard.

Signature GEORGE ARMSTRONG.

Was it a truthful and honest statement, or simply the words of a desperate man, who would say anything to try and save his own life? Sadly, we will never know the answer.

Chapter Ten
Ernie Chapman – Agent Zigzag/Frizchen

Edward Arnold Chapman was born in Burnopfield, County Durham, on 16 November 1914. Nobody then would have guessed that he would go on to play such an important role in the Allied victory in the Second World War.

In 1932 he enlisted in the British Army and became a Guardsman in the 2nd Battalion, Coldstream Guards. During his service he was stationed at the Tower of London. But his military service didn't last long, and it certainly wasn't one that he could have been proud of, as it resulted in him being court-martialled for overstaying his leave by two months. Most of this time he had spent in Soho, London, drinking, partying and doing a few odd jobs, to help pay for the lifestyle he had begun to enjoy. He was sentenced to three months in a military prison which he served at Aldershot in Hampshire, after which he was dishonourably discharged from the service.

On his release from prison, far from changing his ways, he returned to Soho and set out on a life of crime and became a 'safe blower' teaming up with other criminals. His life became one of clubs, drinking, women and more crime, which is how he paid for the lifestyle that he had come to enjoy.

Chapman and his gang committed crimes the length of the country, but the problem for them was that the authorities knew the crimes they were committing and were on to them. They even made the newspapers. Chapman was finally arrested in Jersey and given a two-year sentence, by which time it was March 1939. The sentence he would have received if he had been arrested in Britain would have been much more severe. Only a few months into his sentence Chapman escaped, albeit for a very short time, before being recaptured. This cost him a further year on his sentence.

When German forces occupied the Channel Islands on October 1941, Chapman was still incarcerated in a Jersey prison. It was soon after this that Chapman went to see the German authorities, telling them of his criminal past and offering his services to the German secret service, but nothing came of it. On his release he worked with a black-market gang, out of the back of a barber's shop in St Helier. He had met some of its members whilst in prison.

Sometime in either late 1941 or early 1942 Chapman and another man by the name of Faramus were arrested at the barber's shop in St Helier and put on a boat to Granville in France. Whether Chapman understood why he was being taken to France is unclear. Saint-Denis Internment Camp on the outskirts of Paris was their first destination, and from there they were moved on to Fort de Romainville Prison and Transit Camp at Les Lilas.

Chapman was released from custody at Romainville on 26 April 1942, but only after numerous visits from uniformed German officers. These men turned out to be from the *Abwehr*, and the reason Chapman had been released was because he had agreed to work for them. He was taken to Le Bourget in France, to begin his espionage training. When he had successfully completed his training, he was given the code name of 'Fritz', large sums of money, and was put up in a chateau, where he stayed until the Germans needed him. It would appear that Chapman's reason behind working for the *Abwehr* was nothing to do with believing in Nazi doctrine, but for the money, the lifestyle and the adventure.

His first mission came along in December 1942 when he was parachuted into England with the intention of setting off an explosion at the De Havilland aircraft factory in Hatfield where they built the De Havilland Mosquito aircraft for the Royal Air Force. The Mosquito was used as a bomber and for reconnaissance and submarine hunting.

Chapman arrived in England on 16 December 1942, having been flown across the English Channel in a converted Focke-Wulf bomber with enough room inside for him to be able to parachute from the aircraft. With him he had £1,000 in different currencies, a pistol, and a cyanide capsule. On exiting the aircraft, Chapman became wedged in the hatch, and had to do a fair bit of wriggling to get himself free. Because of the extra time it took him to get out of the aircraft, he missed his intended target and landed near the village of Littleport, Cambridgeshire.

What neither Chapman nor the *Abwehr* were aware of, was that MI5 knew of his arrival as they had long since managed to crack German secret codes. Chapman's aircraft was being shadowed by planes from the RAF's Fighter Command, so a rough idea of where he was likely to land was easy to ascertain. The plan was that once the specific location had been identified, local Police would be alerted so that they could carry out an area search to capture him, they having been informed that they were looking for a deserter from the British Army.

In fact it didn't really matter where he landed, as by then he had already made up his mind that he wasn't going to go ahead with the mission and instead he immediately handed himself in to the local police officer, and asked him to contact British intelligence, which the officer did. Chapman was collected by members of the security service and taken to Camp 020 at Latchmere House in south west London where he was interrogated. At the beginning of the war MI5's headquarters was at Wormwood Scrubs prison.

He appears to have been quite an astute character and was quick to make a deal with his MI5 interrogators. He told them that he would become a double agent for them if all pre-war charges against him were dropped and they readily accepted the deal. Chapman's case officer, Ronnie Reed wrote in his report:

> In our opinion, Chapman should be used to the fullest extent, he genuinely means to work for the British against Germans. By his courage and resourcefulness he is ideally fitted to be an agent.

He was thought suitable to be used as part of the Double-Cross system and was given the code name 'Zigzag', due to what his interrogators had deemed to be an erratic personal history. Chapman was well known to the police, and their records showed that he had used a number of aliases throughout his criminal career.

Chapman's intended target, the De Havilland factory at Hatfield, had a suitably faked sabotage incident take place on the night of 29/30 January 1943, which was so convincing that even aerial photographs taken by German reconnaissance aircraft could not tell that it was anything other than real. But although Chapman didn't really achieve his mission, he had to be able to prove how he had gone about it, as he would certainly be questioned in some detail by the Germans. He also had to decide in which building he was going to detonate his bomb, but even more crucial than that, he first had to acquire some explosives as he hadn't been supplied any by his *Abwehr* contact. MI5 could have quite easily supplied him with some, but that could have worked against him, as it would still be an aspect of the mission he would have to describe in detail. He located an explosives store at a quarry at Sevenoaks in Kent.

The elaborate plan was carried out late in the evening and resulted in the power room having part of its roof blown off, with a number of smoke bombs being let off. The workers, none of whom were in on the ploy, were told that there had been an unexplained explosion in the power room. To help reinforce this story, MI5 also had a story about the incident published in the *Daily Express* newspaper.

Part of the deal the *Abwehr* had struck with Chapman required him to return to France within two and a half months of having carried out his mission. If he didn't want to be blown as a double agent he had no option but to return. But for some reason when he made contact with his contact in Germany, requesting extraction, they were not prepared to help him return. MI5 was certainly keen for him to return because, as a trusted asset of the *Abwehr*, he could be used to gleam important information about the Germans which would be extremely useful to the Allied war effort.

Chapman got himself a job as a steward on a merchant marine ship that sailed from Liverpool to Lisbon in Portugal. The Germans were very impressed with their new agent and what he had achieved at their behest. He ended up in an *Abwehr* safe house in German-occupied Norway. One of the plaudits he was supposedly given was the award of the Iron Cross, making him the only British civilian to have been awarded it – if he was ever awarded it. The Iron Cross was a military award for German military personnel but Hitler had also created the War Merit Cross as a replacement for the non-combatant version of the Iron Cross. This is more likely to be the decoration that Chapman was awarded.

Whilst in Norway he was employed as an instructor helping to train other *Abwehr* agents in Oslo. In Norway he met Dagmar Lahlum and they became romantically involved and very close, so close in fact, that Chapman took a massive risk and revealed to Dagmar that he was a British agent. Fortunately for him Dagmar was a member of the Norwegian resistance. She was happy to discover that he was not a German officer after all and they worked together and gathered information about German military personnel and their activities.

It was not until 29 June 1944, some three weeks after the D-Day landings, that Chapman returned to England. He arrived by parachute and landed in the Cambridgeshire countryside. His mission on that occasion was to report on accuracy and damage that was being caused by Germany's V1 and V2 rockets that were raining down on London and the south-east of England. He sent back positive wireless messages with the news that most of the rockets were hitting their intended targets, when in fact they were not. Many of them fell well short of where they were meant to have landed. This resulted in fewer civilian lives being lost and less damage to homes and businesses.

On his return to England, it wasn't long before he was getting up to his old tricks of hanging out in bars and clubs in Soho and the West End of London and associating with old friends, many of whom were involved in criminality. MI5 was becoming concerned about his behaviour and conduct, making it more difficult to control him. With MI5 at its wits end as to what to do with Chapman, they decided to let him go, and on 2 November 1944, they dismissed him, giving him a total pay off of £7,000, which included £1,000 of the money that he had been given by the Germans. This would be worth somewhere in the region of £385,000 today.

Eddie Chapman had a long and varied life. Opinions about him will vary, but he served his country in its time of need, doing his bit for the British and Allied war effort.

Conclusion

It is unquestionable that MI5's 'Double-Cross' system played a massively important role in the British and Allied war effort. It quite clearly saved many lives as well as reducing the length of the war, although by how much, can be no more than a guess.

War is a dangerous business for all concerned, but it would be interesting to know just how many of the *Abwehr* agents who were captured on their arrival in Britain, would have carried on with their espionage for Nazi Germany if they hadn't been captured. Whatever their reason was for initially agreeing to spy for Germany, and no matter how good or bad a spy they were, they must have also been brave individuals, as it could not have escaped them that if they were captured there was every possibility that they would have been executed for spying. Once captured they must have thought it was all over for them, so when they were given the opportunity by MI5 to become double agents, the relief would have been palpable, though the future uncertain. Some would have still had a feeling of foreboding, thinking about what would happen to them after they no longer served any purpose for the British. The stress they must have all been under whilst contemplating their own fate, must have been all consuming at times.

However, once MI5 had captured all of the *Abwehr* agents, found out what their mission was, and stripped them of all of their relevant and useful knowledge, one wonders why didn't they just execute them? Nobody would have known. This would of course, only have worked if future correspondence between the agents and their handlers in Germany had been via wireless transmissions.

The Gestapo had absolutely no qualms when it came to torturing, then despatching British agents to meet their Maker. They were brutal when it came to the different methods of pain and torture which they liked to inflict upon their victims, showing no remorse for them, rather wallowing in the suffering and death that they caused.

From what we know of the Second World War, those spies who worked for German military intelligence who were captured in Britain, fared much better, mainly due to the Double-Cross system, than did Allied spies who were captured in Nazi-occupied Europe.

Most, if not all of them had been normal civilians before the war, carrying out all kinds of routine, run of the mill jobs, and when the war began and MI5 came calling, those who took up the challenge carried out a very important role for the nation. They had to learn new skills and abilities. Many of them were fluent in languages such as Spanish and German, some were businessmen who had contacts all over Europe and knew their way around. Others were mathematicians who were used at such establishments as the famous Bletchley House, who worked tirelessly on deciphering and breaking German codes. Some of them were just as effective doing what they were doing, as a soldier was fighting on the battlefield.

Sources

www.ancestry.co.uk

Wikipedia

The Spy in the Tower – The untold story of Josef Jakobs the last person to be executed in the Tower of London. (Giselle K. Jakobs)

www.jjtoner.com

www.spyculture.com

www.ww2today.com

www.history.com

The Smithsonian magazine

Secret Wars: One Hundred Years of British Intelligence inside MI5 and MI6. (Gordon Thomas)

www.capitalpunishmentuk.org

www.uboat.net

www.irishtimes.com

www.in2013dollars.com

About the Author

Stephen is a retired Police officer having served with Essex Police as a Constable for thirty years between 1983 and 2013. Both his sons, Luke and Ross, were members of the armed forces, collectively serving five tours of Afghanistan between 2008 and 2013. Both were injured on their first tour. This led to Stephen's first book *Two Sons in a Warzone – Afghanistan: The True Story of a Father's Conflict*, which was published in October 2010.

Both of his grandfathers served in and survived the First World War, one with the Royal Irish Rifles, the other in the Merchant Navy, whilst his father served in the Royal Army Ordnance Corps during the Second World War.

Stephen corroborated with one of his writing partners, Ken Porter, on a book published in August 2012, *German POW Camp 266 – Langdon Hills*, which spent six weeks as the number one best-selling book in Waterstones, Basildon between March and April 2013. Steve and Ken collaborated on a further four books in the Towns & Cities in the Great War series by Pen and Sword. Stephen has also written other titles in the same series of books, and In February 2017 his book, *The Surrender of Singapore – Three Years of Hell 1942-45*, was published. This was followed in March 2018 by *Against All Odds: Walter Tull, the Black Lieutenant*, and in January 2019, *A History of the Royal Hospital Chelsea – 1682 - 2017 – The Warrior's Repose*, which he wrote with his wife, Tanya. They have also written two other books together.

Stephen has also co-written three crime thrillers which were published between 2010 and 2012, which centre round a fictional detective, named Terry Danvers.

When not writing, Tanya and Stephen enjoy the simplicity of walking their four German Shepherd dogs early each morning, at a time when most sensible people are still fast asleep in their beds.

Index

Schutz, Gunther, 55
Scott-Ford, Duncan, 39, 115–19
Sea Eagle, Operation, 78
Seagull, Operation. 77
Sealion, Operation, 60, 62–3, 66
Seraph, HMS, 30
Sergueiew, Nathalie, 33, 35–6, 56
Sicherheitsdienst, 33
Simoes, Ernesto, 57
Smelkov, Yuri, 53
Somervell, Sir Donald, 6
Sostaric, Eugen, 54
Stephens, Lieutenant-Colonel
   Robin 'Tin Eye', 27, 30, 38, 40
Stevenson, Major Melford, 115
Sullivan, Gerda, 52

Terradellas, Josef, 54
Timmerman, Alphonse, 55,
   107–108

Thomsen, Petur, 46
Thummel, Paul, 71
Treachery Act 1940, 1, 4, 6–8, 106,
   110, 114

van den Kieboom, 1–2, 4, 8, 99
Vanhove, Joseph Jan, 113–14
von Harlem, 86
von Janowski, Werner, 39, 58
von Kotze, 55
von Stauffenberg, Claus, 64

Waldberg, Jose, 1–2, 4–5, 7–8, 99
Walti, Werner Heinrich, 99
Weber-Drohl, Ernst, 75
Whale, Operation, 78
Williams, Gwilym, 53
Winter, Franciscus Johannes, 109

Zeiss, Stefan, 59